Elizabethan Stage
Conditions

Elizabethan Stage Conditions

A STUDY OF THEIR PLACE
IN THE INTERPRETATION OF
SHAKESPEARE'S PLAYS

BY

M. C. BRADBROOK

*Professor of English
in the University of Cambridge*

THE HARNESS PRIZE ESSAY, 1931

CAMBRIDGE
AT THE UNIVERSITY PRESS
1968

PUBLISHED BY
THE SYNDICS OF THE CAMBRIDGE UNIVERSITY PRESS

Bentley House, 200 Euston Road, London, N.W. 1
American Branch: 32 East 57th Street, New York, N.Y. 10022

Standard Book Numbers:
521 07215 8 clothbound
521 09539 5 paperback

Library of Congress Catalogue Card No.: 68-30950

First published 1932
First paperback
edition 1968

First Printed in Great Britain at the University Press, Cambridge
Reprinted in Great Britain by Hazell Watson & Viney Ltd,
Aylesbury, Bucks

CONTENTS

521

NOTE

The rash and conjectural nature of much of this essay will sufficiently testify that it is not greatly indebted to other writers. I have drawn chiefly on the work of Sir Edmund Chambers, on *Shakespeare's England*, and the volume on *Shakespeare's Theatre* by members of the Shakespeare Association. The chapter on acting is especially indebted to articles in the last volume by Miss M. St Clare Byrne, Dr G. B. Harrison, and J. Isaacs; and to the work of Archer and W. J. Lawrence.

I am well aware that in many chapters, particularly the one on textual criticism, I have discussed technical questions of which I cannot claim more than a general knowledge, and have commented on the work of scholars to whose learning I can make no pretence. The necessity of relating their work to the study of stage conditions in general will, I hope, serve as an excuse for the attempt, and the bold and speculative nature of modern Shakespearean criticism as a justification for its temerity.

M. C. B.

NOTE ON THE
SECOND IMPRESSION

After thirty years, I find little in my first book that I really want to discard. Chapter III and Chapter IX are now of historic rather than current interest. The position about staging remained where the generation of Chambers established it until the forties, when G. R. Kernodle and Walter Hodges, followed by Richard Southern, Glynne Wickham, and Richard Hosley brought in a practical sense of the theatre and developed wider historic connections with pageantry and the arts. The modern view of the Elizabethan stage is more tentative; we know that we do not know. Some would now abolish the notion of an inner stage altogether. But not only has a practical knowledge of the living theatre enriched scholarship; Elizabethan stages have actually been constructed on which Shakespeare's plays may be acted.

A far-reaching development in bibliography, mainly the work of Fredson Bowers and his pupils, makes this subject so technical that I would now scarcely dare to embark upon it. Here again, views are divided. Fortunately the student of Shakespeare enjoys two means of keeping up to date—*Shakespeare Quarterly*, published since 1950 by the Shakespeare Association of America; and *Shakespeare Survey*, published annually since 1948 under the general editorship of Allardyce Nicoll by the Cambridge University Press. Volume 12 deals with the theatre.

A personal confession to conclude. Some sentences in this essay may sound less than just to that great Shakespearean, Harley Granville Barker. When as a youthful student I wrote them, I knew that Granville Barker was one of the adjudicators for the Harness Prize, and was determined not to curry favour. So I slapped the examiner. I have not forgotten his genial kindness then, and would like to say now how much I have always admired his work.

M. C. BRADBROOK

CAMBRIDGE
May 1962

Chapter I

INTRODUCTION

THE justification of a study of the particular conditions under which Shakespeare's plays were produced is necessarily connected with that of historic criticism in general. In the consideration of most literary works the double question of sources and of biographic facts will usually arise; but the drama differs from other literary forms in that it has a further modifying influence, the contemporary conditions of presentation, to which it is even more closely and inevitably related. Opinion differs as to the value of the biographic approach to literature (it is in any case at its most tenuous in the dramatist). To connect outward events and poetry in the relation of cause and effect is clearly impossible, and the most distinguished of Shakespeare's biographers insists on the impersonality of his art. For him "biography exists to satisfy a natural instinct in man, the commemorative instinct...". "To refuse to interest oneself in a great author's history or personality is almost to defy a natural instinct, which impels inquiry

[1]

about those who prove themselves benefactors. We are not endeavouring to satisfy trivial curiosity. If we go the right way to work, biographic research may be the best form that a tribute of admiration and affection can take ".[1] For Sir Sidney Lee biography seems a tribute to a personality rather than a weapon of criticism, more sightly and more lasting but not more relevant than a public statue.

The value of the study of literary sources is one that has been assailed again and again, from Croce to Wilson Knight. The direct application may be of little use, but as a means of measuring the way in which the author's interests work, by enabling us to see where he has modified and where he has merely absorbed, such knowledge is a most necessary critical weapon. It may also serve an elucidatory purpose by explaining irrelevancies and inconsistencies which result from an assumption of certain facts that are contained in the sources but not carried over into the work. This is especially likely to happen when a dramatist uses old theatrical material. Though we

[1] Sidney Lee, " Principles of biography " and "Impersonal aspect of Shakespeare's Art", in *Elizabethan and other Essays*.

cannot but regard much of the ambiguity of motive in *Hamlet* as deliberate, it would not have puzzled an Elizabethan audience, who would naturally transfer explanations from the old play which they knew.

Such justifications as these will apply also to the study of stage conditions. It is a curious fact that this, the latest to be studied, should be the most indisputably direct influence upon the plays. The eighteenth century retailed anecdotes of Shakespeare's life—with no very serious purpose—and was desultorily interested in his sources. The nineteenth century investigated both very fully, but it is only during the last thirty years that a detailed investigation of stage conditions has been carried out. Malone had opened up the field, but he found few followers.

The separation of historic criticism from appreciative study is one which the writers of both kinds acknowledge. A great deal of work on it is "mere archaeology": far from the plays being the object of the investigation, they are only its instruments, classed with the Swan drawing as data. Chambers repudiates "their literary aspect, with which I am not concerned".[1]

[1] Introduction, *The Elizabethan Stage.*

[3]

Historic criticism, to be of value, must aim at providing an efficient weapon to be used by others and applied with differing results by different people, and therefore the critic is bound to efface himself in the scholar. Yet the distinction leads to abuses: "research, though toilsome, is easy"; and while there is evidence enough elsewhere that the suppression of critical comment is no sign of critical incompetence in Sir Edmund Chambers, it is difficult to muster sufficient credulity to believe the same of all historic investigators.

Writers of appreciative criticism who neglect the historic approach are liable to blunder on questions of tone; to mistake conventions for faults, to rationalise an illogical custom of the theatre, or to miss the point of a device. Raleigh's remark that "those who study Shakespeare in a philosophical vacuum" may mistake for fundamental features of his style the local customs of his theatre, is not quite accurate, for the proof and test of Shakespeare's genius lie precisely in that he hardly bowed to a single exigency, or utilised a single stage device without making it an integral part of the play: so that of both necessities and conveniences he makes virtues. So perfectly is this done that it is possible to read Shakespeare without being forcibly reminded of the local conditions for which he wrote; which could not be said of any other Elizabethan dramatist. Not that he was less of his time than they, but because he possessed greater skill in selecting and judgment in co-ordinating his devices. Hence the study of Elizabethan stage conditions is more essential for the bare understanding of his fellows than of Shakespeare, in that it elucidates them much more: but in Shakespeare's case it allows us to measure much more carefully his power in shaping his inevitable material. The knowledge of Shakespeare's *données* shows how easy and complete was his control, since it is by the merest turn of the wrist that he achieves the transformation (the versification of North's account of Volumnia's plea to her son is the stock example). To transform with the minimum of alteration or distortion in the material is the sign of the great artist.

But perhaps the chief value of the knowledge of stage conditions is a negative one. It prevents wrong assumptions, or the laying of emphasis in the wrong place. This unobtrusive correcting of

the critical focus is almost impossible to define
or describe, like the change of vision produced
by wearing glasses. We may point to particular
places: the irrelevance of a moral judgment of
single characters, particularly of stock types, like
Bertram of Roussillon in *All's Well* (compare
Young Charley in *The Wise Woman of Hogsdon*);
the refusal to expect logical motivation; the
accepting of conventions for some of the soliloquies (*not* the framing a law of the Objective
Truth in Soliloquy). It is largely a question of
tact and unconscious balance, because it was so
in Shakespeare himself. The Elizabethan stage
had no rules: even those tacitly observed, like
Lawrence's law of re-entry, may never have
been conscious, much less formulated. The fact
that investigators have to reconstruct what the
dramatists merely accepted tends to make them
more conscious of their formulae. It is only
when the various conventions of stage, actor
and playwright can be accepted automatically
that knowledge reacts fruitfully upon interpretation.

Chapter II

SHAKESPEAREAN CRITICISM—
EIGHTEENTH AND NINETEENTH
CENTURIES

THE homogeneous character of Restoration and early eighteenth-century criticism has long been recognised. The earlier critics (Dryden, for example) must have been conversant with the conditions of the Elizabethan stage, verbal traditions of which still survived; but their anxiety to dissociate themselves from what appeared to be a more barbarous age would not allow them to recognise it. Critics were not at a sufficient distance to be impartial, and their attitude was as little disinterested as the contemporary one towards Ibsen. Since the earlier stage was generally condemned, its traditions were soon forgotten; and his admirers considered that the happiest service they could perform for Shakespeare was to bring him up to date. It was the period of stage adaptations, and Rowe's first duty as an editor was to introduce a complete system of act and scene division to correspond with that in use on the stage.

[7]

But though the Elizabethan stage was not studied, it remained useful as an excuse for Shakespeare's supposed faults. He was relieved of all responsibility, which was laid upon the unreformed characters of the stage, as well as on the deficiencies of his time in learning and manners. His profession had forced Shakespeare to mix with Players rather than Gentlemen, and therefore, according to Pope, prevented his acquiring taste and polish. A lack of investigation made such general shelving of responsibility easy. Even those who defended Shakespeare's judgment, Howard and Temple, did not do so on historic grounds.

The contemporary standards of constructive excellence, though generally thought absolute in their value, were therefore not to be applied to Shakespeare, who was admitted to have reformed his rude stage as far as unassisted genius might do so:

If we examine the greatest part of these plays by those Rules which were established by Aristotle, and taken from the model of the Greek stage, it would not be a very hard Task to find a great many Faults: but as Shakespeare lived under a kind of mere light of Nature, and had never been made acquainted with the regularity of those precepts, so it would be hard to judge him by a law he knew nothing of. We are to consider him as a man that lived in a state of almost universal licence and ignorance...it cannot but be a matter for wonder that he advanced dramatic poetry as far as he did.[1]

Though by special grace Shakespeare was exempted from the Rules, he could be allowed no alternative theory: an awkward dissociation was the only solution, for it was usually admitted that irregular Beauties were preferable to the exactitude of the Rules, and that "Strength and Nature made amends for Art". (A parallel case is Johnson's defence of Milton's metrical licences.) Shakespeare's age was all that could save him from the Rules and the critics from the problem of choosing between them; so it was invaluable.

The early eighteenth century played "follow my leader" in the matter of appreciative criticism. Dryden's panegyric was the general model; his points were repeated and developed, but not augmented. Textual criticism concerned only primary emendations of the sense, and left no room for examination of structure. The chief

[1] Rowe, *Preface to Shakespeare*.

subject of controversy was the extent of Shakespeare's classical learning; for since the classics provided the rules and models which were the foundations of good writing, it was of the first importance to know if they had been accessible to Shakespeare.

This controversy led up to Farmer's essay (1762), which was of less value in settling the particular point than in showing how much light might be thrown on the text by a study of Elizabethan literature. Hitherto the adaptors had had the best of it; it had been easy for Pope to be ribald about exactitude—"All they want is spirit, taste, and sense". About this time an interest in Shakespeare's sources began to develop also. In 1792 Malone produced his *Historic Account of the Rise and Progress of the English Stage, and of the Oeconomy and Usages of the Ancient Theatres in England*. This provided a scholarly and reasonably full account of the form and customs of the Elizabethan theatre (its most serious slip was in the notion of curtains to the forestage). But though they were widely known, Malone's investigations were not applied directly to the plays. He himself would quote Dekker or Greene to elucidate a corrupt passage, but he did not explain difficulties of construction by a reference to stage conditions. Also the general contempt for Shakespeare's contemporaries remained; his opening pages testify to it sufficiently. A little earlier, Johnson had been quite ignorant of Marlowe, and had thought "Gorboduc" typical of the pre-Shakespearean stage.

Nearly every critic had declared Shakespeare's primary power to be in showing the passions; this accounted for the individuality of his characters, "because it has been proved that confused Passions make indistinguishable Characters".[1] Caliban was the stock example of a convincing character who owed nothing to the Imitation of Nature. It was therefore natural that the first type of appreciative criticism to replace the general panegyric should be the examination of the dramatis personae, still rather as species than as individuals. Warton's papers on *The Tempest* and *King Lear* inaugurated the movement which led up through Kames, Richardson and Morgann to the work of the Romantics. It gradually became customary to regard the dramatis personae as "rather historic than dramatic beings, and when occasion

[1] Dryden, *Grounds of Criticism in Tragedy.*

requires, to account for their conduct from the whole of the character, from general principles, from latent motives, and from policies not avowed".[1] Hence the characters ceased to be theatrical types, and became individuals. Shakespeare had at least been hitherto connected with a stage of sorts; but the later eighteenth century, dissatisfied with the travesties that appeared on the boards, tended less and less to think of Shakespeare in terms of the stage. They could conceive of no other stage but their own; Shakespeare's was still thought of as something crude and bare, with nothing to compensate for its scenic poverty.

Coleridge, Hazlitt and Lamb, therefore, all three rejected the stage. They did not relish Lear as a "tottering old man with a walking stick",[2] and Hamlet, deprived of an adequate forestage, had to hurl his soliloquies at the audience. Coleridge said, "He never saw any of Shakespeare's plays acted but with a degree of pain, disgust and indignation.... He was therefore not distressed at the enormous size and monopoly of

[1] Morgann, *Essay on the Dramatic Character of Sir John Falstaff* (note).
[2] *On the Tragedies of Shakespeare.*

the theatres, which drove Shakespeare from the stage to find his proper place in the heart and the closet, where he sits with Milton enthroned on a two-headed Parnassus ".[1] The "glare of the scenes, with every object realised" bewildered him.

Hazlitt, though he was interested in the virtuosity of the actor, agreed with Lamb and Coleridge. He talked of "Mr Kean's Hamlet" or "Mr Edwards' Richard II", but "Poetry and the theatre do not agree together: the attempt to reconcile them fails not only of effect, but of decorum.... The ideal has no place upon the stage...that which is merely an airy shape, a dream, a passing thought immediately becomes an unmanageable reality.... Thus in the play, Bottom's head is no illusion caused by fairy spells...."[2] This last is parallel to Lamb's timid shrinking from Othello's colour; but the main position is the dislike of a representational stage, and the inability to conceive of any other. The Romantics, had they known Shakespeare's theatre, might not have despaired of the stage;

[1] Lectures of 1813–14, Lecture 5.
[2] *Short View of the English Stage*—"*A Midsummer Night's Dream*".

[13]

but at the very moment when appreciative criticism had become sufficiently particularised to require the help of historic investigation, the two separated. Coleridge certainly advocated the historic method, and seems always trembling on the verge of relating Shakespeare to his age; but he never gets past the Greek stage and the Miracle play. His historical knowledge was neither detailed nor extensive; he had read Malone; he knew the plays of Jonson, Beaumont and Fletcher, and Massinger. On the whole, he too condemns Shakespeare's age and stage by implication ("A naked room, a blanket for a curtain"). It apparently never occurred to him that a naked room might make a suitable background for Shakespeare.

Coleridge and Hazlitt established finally the critical approach through the characters, and their method persisted throughout the nineteenth century. Appreciative criticism was deflected from the work towards psychology and ethics, and the antithesis of learning and taste was stronger than it had ever been in the eighteenth century, though "sense" vacillated from one side to the other, and was not too ready to appear on either hand. Coleridge and German criticism, which had largely percolated through him, set the style for appreciative work.

Nineteenth-century criticism, influenced no doubt by the cult of the novel, neglected Shakespeare's dramatic qualities consistently. The numerous books on his *Mind and Art* or his *Dramatic Art* considered him solely as a delineator of character, or related his plays to a central moral precept. Dowden compared him at length with Bacon, Hooker, Raphael and Michael Angelo, but in the first twenty-five pages of his book there are only three quotations from the text. So far was Shakespeare separated from the stage that much of the inferior criticism was only a kind of mental performance of each play by the critic, at which the reader attended. Emotion was underlined, appearances and behaviour of various characters described, and their inner sensations suggested, exactly as any competent actor might do. "Juliet turns her pale face appealingly on her father"[1] replaced "We must assume that at this point Juliet grows pale". It was doubtless a satisfactory arrangement which allowed middle-aged gentlemen to play Mercutio if they wished, or to roar a lusty Othello.

[1] Dowden.

Meanwhile, the scholars had begun their researches into biography. The work of J. O. Halliwell-Phillipps produced a crop of imitative and inferior biographies in the 'fifties. The degree of general interest in this work is attested by the fact that it received the compliment of parody. As Steevens and Malone had called up the forger Ireland from the vasty deep, the inevitable response of Supply to Demand, so the Baconians and Oxfordians appeared, followed by those minor eccentrics who merely wished to prove that Shakespeare was a cripple, or a lawyer, or a sailor, or a bee-keeper at some period of his existence.

It was not till the close of the century that biographic research began to affect appreciative criticism; but Frank Harris appeared hard on the heels of Sidney Lee, and the critic relinquished the rôle of hero to Shakespeare himself. The establishment of the chronological sequence of the plays (begun by Malone, but completed by the "internal tests" of Furnivall and his colleagues of the New Shakspere Society) allowed more play to the Moral Critic, and Shakespeare appeared in the full panoply of his Four Periods.

Shakespeare as a dramatist was completely forgotten. Swinburne, for instance, usually referred to his works as "poems". A scene in Shakespeare meant no more than a "scene" in Dickens. The fact that the performances went on within the heads of the critics tended to make the plays seem more like novels, for the filling-out of a full situation was done by means of words, and not by means of direct presentation or, as it should be in true reading, by a single and unformulated response, which is only to be analysed retrospectively.

The eighteenth century used its own ignorance of Shakespeare's stage as a means of avoiding the discrepancies between his practice and the neo-classic creed: they were unconsciously interested in remaining ignorant of its details. The Romantics, by their lack of knowledge or interest in his stage, were deprived of the knowledge of a possible substitute for their own unsatisfactory stage, and so were led to divorce Shakespeare's plays from the theatre. This tendency persisted throughout the nineteenth century, though it was reinforced by outside influence; the Nonconformist Conscience, for instance, which could produce the Family Shakespeare, might have had something to do with the segregation of Shakespeare from the immorality of the theatres.

Chapter III

SHAKESPEAREAN CRITICISM—
TWENTIETH CENTURY

THE positivist and realist temper of the twentieth century showed itself first of all in the production of histories and reconstructions of the Elizabethan stage, since the prime necessity was to collect and arrange the data, before it could be directly applied to Shakespeare's plays. Sir Edmund Chambers began his researches in 1904 with the publication of *The Medieval Stage*. In the same year C. Brodmeier published his *Shakespeare's Stage According to the Old Stage Directions*, and articles by W. J. Lawrence on detailed points of staging began to appear in various periodicals. The alternationist theory, which Brodmeier propounded, was the result of the exhilaration of new discoveries operating on an insufficient amount of material; and admirably illustrates the danger of applying scientific methods in the expectancy of discovering scientific facts, a procedure about as logical as digging with a silver spade in the hope of striking a vein of silver. American scholarship found this type of investigation very much to its taste; and the studies of G. F. Reynolds and V. E. Albright appeared in 1905 and 1907 respectively. Meanwhile, Feuillerat and Wallace were investigating the history of the private theatres and the Court entertainments (*Bureau de Menus Plaisirs*, 1910; *First London Theatre*, 1913) and Chambers published some of the material which was later to be incorporated in *The Elizabethan Stage*. In 1911 and 1913 Lawrence issued his *Elizabethan Playhouse* (1st and 2nd Series), collections of essays on detailed points of structure and presentation. Sidney Lee's new edition of his *Life* incorporated a good deal of the new material; A. H. Thorndike's *Shakespeare's Theatre* appeared in 1916; and J. Quincy Adams, another American scholar, published his *Shakespeare's Playhouses* in 1917. There was a temporary lull in the books on staging until in 1924 *The Elizabethan Stage* appeared, the scope and comprehensiveness of which seems to have reduced the lesser spirits to silence. It is still possible to glean after Chambers' reaping; and there is, of course, plenty of work to be done on the later stage. Lawrence's studies of such things as stage traps, properties and prompt books continued to appear and, in 1927, a fruitful year for Shakespearean studies, he published *Pre-Restoration Stage Studies*.

This pure stage history was not specifically related to Shakespeare, though his name appears so frequently on the title-pages of books. The earlier and more speculative studies make amusing reading now, with their furious discussions of the "place behind the stage", and their attempts to reconcile the De Witt drawing with a general theory that should apply to all public theatres.

The investigation of Shakespeare's dramatic structure and his relationship to his contemporaries was another development of historic research that proved popular, especially with Americans. *Shakespeare's Plots* (Fleming, 1902) and *Shakespeare's Soliloquies* (Arnold, 1911) are typical of the Ph.D. theses, regularly turned out, with perhaps more industry than wit, from the American universities. G. P. Baker's *Shakespeare as a Dramatist* (1907) and Prof. Brander Matthew's *Shakespeare the Dramatist* (1913) were more general studies, which showed that the tendency to approach through the characters rather than the plot was still too strong to be resisted: their suggestions appear naïve and obvious now; and Shakespeare is treated by them purely as a dramatist, and not as a dramatic poet, whereby more than half of his dramatic method is necessarily overlooked.

The growing conviction of the impersonality of Shakespeare's art and the tenuity of its connection with the outward facts of his life was much strengthened by these investigations into stage history and dramatic structure. It was realised with something of a shock that he had had to cater for a particular company and a particular audience, and that apparently he had taken some trouble to do so. The exhilaration of this new discovery meant that it in its turn seemed an explanation of far too much of his work. As he had written the sonnets merely to flatter his patron, so he had written *Hamlet* merely with an eye on the box office. The most offensive popularisation of this creed is Bernard Shaw's, for he represents Shakespeare as a shifty dramatist cadging lines, "Nothing but humours and observation", with snobbery and bumptiousness as his dominating characteristics.

This limitation of Shakespeare's interests was enhanced by the researches into the influence of theatrical fashion upon his plays. This, a kind of offshoot of the study of the stage, led to the recognition that the Elizabethan dramatists formed a school, and had had a certain influence upon one another. The nineteenth century, though it studied the minor Elizabethans, looked on them rather as a collection of individuals; Swinburne, for instance, places each one in austere isolation from his fellows. A. H. Thorndike, in his studies on *The Influence of Beaumont and Fletcher on Shakespeare's Later Plays* and of the Revenge type on *Hamlet*, evolved a method later used by Stoll and others. Popularisation was again dangerous. It was seen that Shakespeare was ready to adapt himself to contemporary tastes, and this was somehow considered a proof that he was therefore necessarily less personally implicated in his plays (an exaltation of Subject over Treatment that seems quite unwarranted). Raleigh rebutted this crude idea vigorously and simply: "They asked for Jew-baiting, and he gave them the *Merchant of Venice*". (The biographic explanation was still reserved for the bitter comedies, which have since been explained on a Sound Scientific Basis by the bibliographers, except *Troilus and Cressida*; but that has not yet appeared in the Cambridge *New Shakespeare*.) The postulation of a direct connection between the following of a fashion and the impersonal character of the plays would not, I think, have been so strong had it not been that the studies of the stage had emphasised the direct dependence of the plays upon its structure.

Bradley, in his *Essay on the Audience* (1909),[1] again related Shakespeare in a different way to his environment. *Shakespeare's England* (1916) was virtually a reconstruction of the tastes and interests of his audience. Bridges developed the influence of the spectators in his essay,[2] where he almost readopted the eighteenth-century expedient of making them scapegoats for all that an alteration of taste and of theatrical convention has made unpalatable to the twentieth-century reader (see Dover Wilson's reply, *The Elizabethan Shakespeare*).[3] Dr Harrison's *Elizabethan Journals* have attempted something of the same task as *Shakespeare's England*, but on a chronological basis.

The influence of the actors has been rather

[1] *Oxford Lectures on Poetry.*
[2] Bridges, *Collected Essays*, 1927.
[3] British Academy Annual Shakespeare Lecture, 1928.

neglected, perhaps because it is much more difficult to reconstruct. The history of the companies has been investigated, and such general questions as the part played by boy actors. T. W. Baldwin, in a detailed study[1] of the Chamberlain-King's men, attempts to "cast" the plays; but Elizabethan histrionics and styles of acting have hardly been tackled at all. Biographies of various actors, such as Mrs Stopes' book on *The Burbages*, are merely biographies.

It is during the last decade that the influence of the stage histories has begun to show itself in appreciative criticism. The theatre has been reconstructed, and the ways of nineteenth-century representationalism abjured—the work of Mr William Poel represents in this respect a practical correlative to the theoretical explorations of scholars. Harley Granville-Barker's *Prefaces to Shakespeare* (1927, 1929) and his *Essay on Dramatic Method* (1931) and the volume on *Shakespeare's Theatre* by members of the English Association (1927) show a more enlightened and temperate relating of Shakespeare to the stage, and are content to elucidate his effects rather

[1] *The Organisation and Personnel of the Shakespearean Company*, 1927.

than to erect them into principles of his policy.

The most interesting development of Shakespearean criticism has been, perhaps, the effect which the study of stage conditions, leading to an emphasis on the structure of the plays, has had upon the nineteenth-century conception of them as primarily studies in characterisation. The new investigations were a little retarded from taking their full effect by the publication of Bradley's *Shakespearean Tragedy*, which, though showing the influence of the new scholarship in the precision and detail of its investigations, followed the methods of Coleridge and Hazlitt. The thoroughness with which it did so was in a sense its own *reductio ad absurdum*, for the number of inconsistencies and irrelevancies that were revealed showed the incongruity of judging Shakespeare by the standards of the novel or the drama of the Shaw-Galsworthy kind, i.e. through consistency of motivation and character, and the logical articulation of the plot. The Americans again took up the question, and the inconsistencies were defended, not on their own value, but by considering the characters as real enough to be explained in terms of dual personality. (It is, perhaps, as well that Behaviourism cut off the Transatlantic retreat into psychological justification by hoisting the cowards with their own petard.) The comparative studies of Stoll (*Othello*, 1916; *Hamlet*, 1919; *Shakespearean Studies*, 1927) again helped to destroy the conception of integrity of character. The researches into the histories of the plays themselves, which disclosed possibilities of wholesale collaboration, revision and interpolation, further complicated matters. Hamlet, the test case for the swing of critical theory, has been explained recently as a man of action (Stoll), an amalgam of two different characters, Kyd's Hamlet plus Shakespeare's (Robertson), an incomplete projection of a certain baffling state of mind in Shakespeare himself (T. S. Eliot), a case of mental shock and paralysis of the will (Clutton Brock), and regular medical melancholia (Henry Somerville, Lily Campbell).

Finally, the detailed study of versification and style doubtless owes something of its severity of method and also its faith in scientific principles to the stage studies. Robertson and Dugdale Sykes clearly owe their methods to Thorndike and the earlier investigators; and less iconoclastic work, such as Miss Spurgeon's pamphlet on *Imagery in Shakespearean Tragedy*, or even so romantic a study as Mr Wilson Knight's *Wheel of Fire*, while divorced from all direct connection with the theatre, shows an approach to each play as a whole and as a play.

Chapter IV

SHAKESPEARE'S STAGE AND HIS
DRAMATIC STRUCTURE

(*Note.* For this Chapter I assume the integrity of the Folio Canon. My chronological sequence is that of Chambers,
William Shakespeare, vol. I, p. 270.)

THANKS to the type of research discussed
in the previous chapter, it is now possible
to reconstruct with fair adequacy the shape
and appearance of Shakespeare's playhouses.
His early plays were written during a period of
theatrical disturbance, and it is not certain for
whom. In 1594 the Chamberlain's men settled
at the Theatre in Shoreditch, where they remained
till 1599, when, owing to a dispute with Henslowe, the owner of the lease, they built the
Globe on the Bankside. Later they acquired a
private playhouse, the Blackfriars, which they
sublet to the Children of the Chapel, until 1609,
when they began to use it themselves. Some of
Shakespeare's last plays were probably designed
for performance there. In addition, his plays
were often given at Court during festivals, and
some of them (*A Midsummer Night's Dream* and

[29]

The Tempest in particular) were written or revised for special occasions. But the greater part of his plays, in the form in which they have survived, are probably Globe productions.

The chief characteristic of the public stage seems to be its neutrality, and its corresponding virtue, flexibility. The Greeks, while they employed a neutral background, were tied by the presence of the chorus, which served as a localising body, and imposed a modified form of the unities. The Elizabethan stage was free from any suggestions of particular locality (the theory that locality boards, of the kind referred to by Sir Philip Sidney and used in the plays of William Percy, were in general use has not found general acceptance). The stage had properties but no scenery; the trees of the popular orchard or woodland set, whether real or not, must have provided rather thin illusion, and this was certainly the most elaborate scene of the early stage. Spectacle replaced scenery; startling but intermittent effects of the kind used in the comic conjuring of *Friar Bacon and Friar Bungay* supplied the demands of the more unsophisticated.

It is probable that the stage effects became much more elaborate towards the end of Shake-

speare's career, and fell little short of those at
Court in gorgeousness. Many of Shakespeare's
plays were of course given at Court before
Elizabeth and James; and the playwright would
probably have to reckon beforehand on the
possibility of his play being given in a Court
setting, for the players received short notice of a
command performance, and usually gave an item
from their repertory.

But in spite of occasional Court performances,
and, at a later period, of Blackfriars' presenta-
tions, Shakespeare's stage remains primarily that
of the Theatre and the Globe; its advantages
and disadvantages, theirs.

The flexibility which we have noted was at
once an invitation to licence. Time and place
could be neglected or telescoped to serve a
dramatic purpose. The "double time" of *Othello*
can be found in almost every play of the Canon,
if it is examined sufficiently closely. Sometimes
it runs through the whole play: sometimes it is
only a matter of a scene or two (*Richard II*, 1. 4,
and 2. 1) or even a single scene (*Cymbeline*, 2. 2)
which begins at "near midnight" and ends at
3 a.m.—but compare Faustus' final soliloquy
and *The Changeling*, 5. 1. In all of these cases the

telescoping is clearly in the interests of the plot and justifies itself against the charge of muddle-headedness by its utility. "Shakespeare knew the value of time, but he knew even more the value of speed."[1]

The Elizabethan habits with regard to locality are even more complicated. There may be a battlefield with two tents side by side at an idealised distance (*Richard II*, 5. 3). The pastoral "Scene individable" of *Love's Labour's Lost* shows the entrance to the king's palace and the princess's tent. There are "split" scenes like *Romeo and Juliet*, 4. 5, and *Measure for Measure*, 3. 1, where the place changes by the opening or shutting of the curtains on the inner stage, transporting the characters on the outer stage to the new locality. There are unlocalised scenes like *1 Henry IV*, 4. 4 (which does not happen anywhere in particular), and a character is often delocalised for a soliloquy (e.g. Iago in *Othello*, 4. 3, a "split" scene). The stage may represent a street leading to the senate house and the senate house itself (*Julius Caesar*, 3. 1) or a long stretch of moorland (*Richard II*, 2. 3; compare *Arden of Feversham*, the scene on Rainham Downs).

[1] M. St Clare Byrne in *Shakespeare's Theatre*.

There are in fact no "scenes" in the sense of separate units, and no locality except where it is indicated in the text. The few localising stage directions, "Enter in the forest of Gaultree" (2 *Henry IV*, 4. 1) or "Scaling ladders at Harfleur" (*Henry V*, 3. 1), are supported by the text. When an important group of characters or when all the characters leave the stage there is a sense of pause, and the prompter drew a line across his copy, while the groundlings probably shifted from one foot to the other.

The question of act division is still one that perplexes the experts. Shakespeare seems to point in both directions: the clumsiness of the interval between Acts 3 and 4 of *Midsummer Night's Dream* suggests no interval, and *Henry V's* Choruses (though the Folio act divisions do not agree with them) favour it. The ambiguous terms of the Induction to *The Malcontent* ("To abridge the not-received custom of music in our theatre") do not help to determine the custom of the Chamberlain's company, but it cannot have been an early habit of the men's theatres to have regular intervals.

To play Shakespeare on a picture stage and with regular intervals is to do as much violence to his stagecraft as Pope did to his versification by attempting to fit it to eighteenth-century standards. It has, however, taken a great deal longer to recognise the first distortion, and it was not till the publication of the Cambridge *New Shakespeare* that the well-meant improvements of act and scene division were abolished in a popular edition of the plays.

The unlocalised drama (to which the modern stage has largely returned) allowed Shakespeare to indulge in loose flowing construction, episodic plots, and complex action. It is responsible for most of those features of his plays which appeared to be faults to the eighteenth century, and for the fact that he was largely unplayable in the nineteenth century. This vagueness of place may have been encouraged by the frequency with which allegorical figures were allowed to move on the same plane as human beings in the plays, which confused the sense of time and place. (Consider Rapine and Murder in *Titus*, and the dumb show in *A Warning for Fair Women*, and all the confusion between Induction and Play in *James IV*, where Bohun often talks of his story as though it were a reality which he was controlling like a god.)

The early plays, written before the formation of the Chamberlain's company in 1594, show a prentice interest in stage mechanics and a reliance on business to carry off a scene. The University wits had been very interested in exploiting the meagre possibilities of their stage: the "place behind the stage" excited them rather as the pumps did Mr Crummles. This was the golden age of drum and trumpet history, of sieges to the music room, of monstrous apparitions shooting up through trap doors, of blazing stars, five moons, and three suns in the heavens.

1 Henry VI is a battle play *par excellence*. The alarums and excursions form the chief interest, there are many sieges, and in the case of the surprisal of Orleans (2. 1), where the French leap the walls in their shirts, the action cuts out any necessity for dialogue. Here, too, use is made of that rare resource, the "top" or third storey of the theatre (3. 2). All the pumps and wash-tubs are in evidence. In *2 Henry VI*, the most loosely constructed of the trilogy, the chief bit of business is the number of times the property head appears. Margaret dangles it in the Court as that of her lover Suffolk, to the mild discomfort of Henry; it also serves as Lord Saye's head (4. 6) and as Cade's (5. 1). The comic scenes are very definitely localised; Cade "strikes his staff on London stone", and the impostor of St Albans is unmasked there. This gives a feeling of naïveté in the handling, when contrasted with the unlocalised Court scenes. Part 3 is again a battle play, but it does not exploit the stage very much; it depends rather on patterned movement like the entries of the Lords (5. 1).

Richard III, except for 5. 3, is fairly simply staged. It, too, depends on patterned entries and grouping; the figures of the queens in the scenes of lament would be arranged conventionally. Clarence's cell would be merely the inner stage; an occasional "state" is needed for Edward or Richard; Richard appears on the balcony between two bishops (3. 7). 5. 3 is rather difficult to construct. The two tents might have been on opposite sides of the stage; or Richmond may have used the inner stage. The ghosts would rise through the trap one by one.

In *Titus Andronicus* the grouping is equally elaborate. The first scene uses the balcony for the senate house; the rivals enter by the side doors and go up through the centre door in turn; the tomb of the Andronici (probably a property like

Juliet's) is shown on the inner stage. The woodland set is used in Act 2, and the trap door forms
the pit into which the Andronici are thrown
after Bassanius' body. In 5. 2 Titus' study is
evidently placed above, for Tamora invites him
to "come down" from it. The method of
representing the mutilations of the various
characters is uncertain; it may have been
horridly realistic (Henslowe possessed property
hands) or merely conventional.

The Taming of the Shrew uses the upper stage to
house the presentors, the usual custom (*The
Spanish Tragedy* is an exception. The presentors
sit on the stage because the balcony is needed for
the stage spectators in the final scene). Here,
however, they fade out in an unexplained manner; the scene at the Pedants (5. 1) only requires
a window, and there were windows over the
side doors, as well as the balcony, so that that
scene cannot explain matters. Perhaps the end
is lost; and Shakespeare in any case remembered
it when he wrote Bottom's speech on his dream.

The Comedy of Errors has little need of elaborate staging to add to its complications. It has
been suggested that the different twins used
different doors, the Syracusans always entering

on the left and the Ephesians on the right, or vice versa. But a simple mark of dress would serve to distinguish them. The same method might have been used in *Twelfth Night* to distinguish Viola and Sebastian.

Mistaken identity is in itself a form of business parallel to the patterned effects of *Richard III*. It concentrates all the attention on the actors, and is therefore eminently suitable for an unpropertied stage.

The Two Gentlemen of Verona is a text so deficient in stage directions that it has been classed among those assembled from players' parts and the "plot". It could be very simply played. Silvia appears at her window once (4. 2), and presumably the woodland set would be used in Act 5.

Love's Labour's Lost, like *The Tempest*, has a "scene individable". Its properties are only the tree which Berowne climbs and Longaville's "bush". The chief interest is again in the complicated minuet danced by the carefully paired-off characters.

Romeo and Juliet is one of the most difficult of Shakespeare's plays with regard to presentation. There is the early scene where the masquers march around the stage before reaching Capulet's house. It has been suggested that this is not a "split" scene, but that round the stage = round the *back* of the stage, i.e. they "go out at one door and come in at another". Then there is the problem of the orchard wall. It is difficult to conceive the scene without a real wall, perhaps thrust on through the middle door, cutting the stage in two. Juliet appears on one side of it at a window, with the orchard set beneath her. It is interesting to note the very obvious parody of this same orchard wall in the rustics' play of *Pyramus and Thisbe*. Friar Lawrence's cell is a further difficulty; the nurse "enters and knocks" on his door (3. 3) and he lets her in and shuts the door. Juliet also has to parley with Paris on the threshold (4. 1). But if the cell were the inner stage (as cells usually are) the door would have to be on the side facing the audience. Chambers suggests an imaginary door. A solution would be to place the cell above, like that of Titus Andronicus; the characters could then enter on the lower stage and go up. This would involve some difficulty, of course, since Romeo is lying on the floor in 3. 3, and he would be concealed by the balcony rails. The same difficulty occurs

in *Antony and Cleopatra*, where the wounded
Antony is hoisted over the rails and dies behind
them. Perhaps they could be temporarily removed. When characters have to leap the walls
it would add greatly to their difficulties if they
had to vault the rails in order to do so.

Juliet's bedchamber shifts from upper to
lower stage in 3. 4. In 4. 3 it seems to be on the
inner stage ("She falls upon her bed within the
curtains"), but there were curtains on the
balcony, too. (See the "removal" of Andrugio's
ghost in *Antonio's Revenge*—though this was
a Paul's play.) At the end of the scene the nurse
delocalises the scene by drawing the curtains;
and the musicians would be conceived to be in
the courtyard. (If the bed were on the upper
stage and they were on the lower, this would be
easier.)

Finally there is the elaborate staging of 5. 2.
The tomb was a property, not merely the inner
stage itself, like that which served for the
Andronici or for Hero. (Compare the one in
The Second Maiden's Tragedy which "flies open
with a great clatter".) Even Elizabethan credulity would have been strained to see Romeo
attack the traverse with a mattock and a spade.

By this time Shakespeare had begun to work his stage effects into the texture of his play. Juliet sees Romeo below "like one dead in the bottom of a tomb". The physical movements are more closely related, through metaphor, to the poetry. Romeo lies on the ground to measure his grave. A feeling for the stage effect is behind Juliet's whisper:

Hist! Romeo, hist! O! for a falconer's voice
To lure this tassel-gentle back again.

Compare her single exclamation to Lawrence after the strain of playing up to Paris' courtesies: "O, shut the door!"

In *Midsummer Night's Dream* Shakespeare was perhaps writing for a private performance. For the first time he has provided his own setting, with the result that every stage setting is cheapened when put against the talk of the fairy to Puck. The sense of time passing is delicately suggested: 3. 2, l. 377, "Night's swift dragons cut the clouds full fast" is followed by

...O long and tedious night,
Abate thy hours! shine comforts from the east!

The fairies depart:

Fairy king, attend and mark:
I do hear the morning lark,

Then the horns wind as day breaks, and the dogs' ears brush the dew off the flowers. The delicacy of movement from grey to full dawn is impossible on a stage whose lighting brightens from half to full strength in a minute, and where time and place are fixed. This passage has a clear connection with the aubade in *Romeo and Juliet*, but there the effect was merely episodic; here it is part of the structure, of the sense of the dissolving of the enchantments of the night. The advance in technique in *Midsummer Night's Dream* has been noted by nearly every critic; the subtle use of song to suggest appropriate background makes it the starting-point for Mr Noble's investigations. An odd relic of realism is the flowery bank where Titania lies. (Henslowe had two among his properties.) By the time of *Hamlet* it had become archaic and was relegated to the play within the play.

The method of *Midsummer Night's Dream* was continued in the middle comedies; song and incidental description replaced an interest in the structural possibilities of the stage. *Richard II*, though a history play, has only one scene on the walls (3. 3), and here the movement is made significant; Richard quibbles on his "coming down" to Henry. The introduction of the garden in 3. 4 gives a kind of relief by insisting on a particular locality and men of a particular occupation after the vaguely placed scenes between soldiers which have preceded it. Again, Shakespeare is experimenting in delicacy of suggestion of place; the sense of a gradual approach to Flint Castle is foreshadowed all through Act 3.

In the comedies and histories of 1596 to 1600 there is practically no exploitation of stage devices. The orchard set is used in *As You Like It*, for the Countess's garden in *Twelfth Night* (3. 4, a "split" scene ending in a street), for Portia's garden in *The Merchant of Venice*; in *2 Henry IV* it is Shallow's orchard, and it reappears in the final scene of *King John*. *The Merchant of Venice* is the most elaborate of the comedies: there are scenes above; the casket scene would need the inner stage; and the senate scene gave opportunity for ceremony. The later *Much Ado about Nothing* has its arbour (a property that served for many plays), and Hero's monument, but there is no elaborate grouping and no use of upper or inner stage. Shakespeare is interested rather in contrasting his main plot and sub-plot, and in the alternation of his patterned early style (*As You Like It*, 5. 2, ll. 90 ff.) with scenes in colloquial prose. Blank verse is abandoned for the more interesting parts of the plays; and when it occurs in large quantities it is uninspired (*2 Henry IV*). These history plays have no drum and trumpet appeal; when in *Henry V* Shakespeare is forced to make some attempt at realism, he does it with dissatisfaction and conscious apology. He was evidently as irritated as Ben Jonson for the moment by the inadequacies of his stage. Although this is a battle play the walls are only used once. The history play, by bringing Shakespeare back to the realism he had found so attractive at the beginning, showed how far he had progressed.

Henry V is the low-water mark of Shakespeare's interest in the stage. With *Julius Caesar* the tide turns (this change coincides with the removal of the Chamberlain's men from the Theatre, and the building of the Globe in 1599). The use of

> ...the restless course
> That time doth run with calm and silent foot

in 2. 1 (see ll. 2–4, 29–40, 101–111, 234–236, 261–263) is the chief instrument in raising suspense and a feeling of the inevitability of the tragedy

(compare the last scene in *Faustus*). The same
method is used at the end, in the keyed-up
expectancy of the men before the battle, and
their overwhelming consciousness of the mere
passage of time:

If we do meet again, why then we'll smile.

It is noticeable that Shakespeare usually stresses
his time at night or early dawn. He had done so
as early as *Richard III* (5. 2), and was to develop
it further in the first act of *Hamlet* and the second
of *Macbeth*.

Julius Caesar is also fairly elaborately staged.
Crowds are more complex than soldiers like
Henry V's; there is a continuous scene (3. 3)
where Caesar goes through the streets to the
senate house (placed, as usual, above). Shakespeare has here developed his habit of slipping
in a short contrasting scene (2. 4) to show the
effect of action on a minor character. It was a
development from the short "breathing space"
scene (*1 Henry IV*, 4. 1).

Hamlet's most elaborate stage mechanics are
connected with the ghost. It appears on, above
and below the stage; it drags the others round
the stage in picturesque groupings to swear

[45]

silence. All through the first act Shakespeare insists on his background: the time of night, the place, the temperature.

The staging of the play within the play is a matter for doubt. Spectators, like presentors, were usually in the gallery, but here the interest is in the audience rather than the play, and Hamlet certainly needs to be below. Perhaps the play was on the inner stage. Ophelia's grave was probably a trap, let half down to show the grave-digger, and the grapple of Hamlet and Laertes.

The bitter comedies show an equal interest in the stage. The confidence with which the armed prologue of *Troilus and Cressida* announces the position at the opening of the play contrasts strongly with the halting apologetics of *Henry V*. The combat between Hector and Ajax was no doubt the biggest piece of spectacle in the play: but such scenes as 1. 2, 2. 3, and 3. 1, ll. 38–74 depend very strongly on the visual impression. *Measure for Measure* shows a return to the comedy technique, especially in the interlude of Marianna in the moated grange.

Othello uses the upper stage (1. 1), the inner stage (1. 3, 4. 2, 4. 3, 5. 1, etc.), crowds are brought on, and there is a senate scene. Here

Shakespeare for the first time uses the curtains of the inner stage to close his action, so that the bodies do not need to be carried off. Iago is often delocalised, e.g. 1. 3, l. 304, 4. 2, l. 173 (the first part of this last scene is in Desdemona's bedroom, the last in a street). The structural device of eavesdropping and three-cornered comment which Shakespeare had used already in *Troilus and Cressida*, 5. 2, he complicates by Othello's inability to hear all, and his consequent misconception of the action (4. 1). There is a parallel to this in Iago's comments on Desdemona and Cassio (2. 1, l. 167), and Othello's remarks as he reads the letter from Venice reproduce Iago's tone exactly (4. 1, ll. 229–274). Both *Hamlet* and *Othello* depend on intrigue far more closely than do *Lear* and *Macbeth*; therefore the "background" is more definite and less important. Othello carries his own picturesque suggestions with him of "antres vast, and deserts idle", and the sun where he was born; but it is personal and does not belong to the play as a whole. Nor is the supernatural in *Hamlet* present all the way through. The second appearance of the ghost, though effective enough, is rather incongruous; like Banquo's ghost after the witches' scenes, it has a certain concreteness and loses its terror when out of "the glimpses of the moon", or "the fog and filthy air".

Lear and *Macbeth* both depend much more closely on their background. The construction of *Lear* is effected through a deliberate blurring of time and space. *Macbeth*, too, is only vaguely located until the end, when, owing to the prophecy about Birnam Wood, references to place become frequent. It was only the bareness of the stage that allowed Shakespeare to introduce the heath scenes in *Lear*, where "the actor impersonates the storm and Lear together", or rather the poetry provides them both. Here the contrasting scenes in the castle reproduce structurally the contrasts of the parallel plot and sub-plot. Shakespeare is introducing spectacle freely now; he brings into *Macbeth* the shows of the witches and Malcolm's soldiers marching with boughs of trees, because he has become sufficiently at home in tragedy to fuse not merely combats (as in *Hamlet*), which are fairly easily related to the action, but his old technique of song (the Fool in *Lear*) and the cruder weapons of show.

Antony and Cleopatra is the most Elizabethan

of all Shakespeare's plays from the point of view of construction. Its whole effect depends upon the sense of the world-wide nature of the struggle. (See Miss Spurgeon's pamphlet, which decides that "world" is the characteristic image of the play.) This effect is gained not only by imagery but by the rapid shift of the scenes, the cinematograph method of showing Antony in Rome and Cleopatra in Egypt, as the cinema shows alternate shots of the struggling heroine and the hero galloping to the rescue. Shakespeare's theatre was very near to the cinema in technique: his trick of showing a series of short separate actions, each one cut off before it is finished (e.g. the battle scenes of *Julius Caesar*) which gives a sense of merged and continuous waves of action, is a common habit of Eisenstein and Pudovkin.

In spite of complexity of movement *Antony and Cleopatra* is simply staged, except for the galley scene and the last act. The exact position of Cleopatra's monument and how she is captured is impossible to determine, owing to the lack of stage directions. In 4. 13 it is certainly above; at the end of 5. 2 certainly below. Shakespeare, again, uses his stage to give an effect of the supernatural, in the eerie scene where the music of the departing Hercules is heard by soldiers in the dawn. It is played under the stage, and the soldiers bewilderedly follow it to and fro, exactly as Hamlet had shifted at the voice of the ghost.

Coriolanus is partly a battle play and so there is a scene before the gates, and the walls are used (1. 4, ll. 12 ff.). The storming is not a simple movement; it is a retreat and a re-advance, and it is used to display Coriolanus' headlong valour and not merely as an interlude. 1. 7 suggests a complicated piece of business, almost a dumb show. But the stage directions for this play are particularly full and detailed. Coriolanus, from the reticent nature of his feelings and his inarticulate nature, gains effect by "entering cursing" or "with his arm in a scarf" just as "I am weary, yea, my memory is tired" has as many implications as though it were directly ironical. And for the climax of the action, Coriolanus, standing with his mother, "holds her by the hand, silent" (5. 3, l. 182). This is a play of massed and processional movement; the state entries of Coriolanus and of Volumnia are balanced by the brawling scenes, for which

Shakespeare provides explicit directions. The crowds are more complicated than those of *Julius Caesar*.

In the Romances Shakespeare was writing for a different stage, the Blackfriars' or the Court; and his attitude to the stage alternates between boredom and experiment. Twice he uses the inner stage for a discovery (*Cymbeline*, 2. 2; *The Tempest*, 5. 1, l. 171) and, in the first case, the whole scene takes place on the inner stage, the unique instance of this in Shakespeare. Prospero appears on the "top", a region unused since *1 Henry VI* (*The Tempest*, 3. 2, l. 16). Shakespeare uses his old devices of the short breathing space (*Winter's Tale*, 3. 1) with new charm; and though he has to use a Chorus to overcome the gap of years, it is not done apologetically. Indeed, it seems to suggest Prospero's famous speech (*The Tempest*, 4. 1, l. 146):

> ...I witness to
> The time that brought them in: so shall I do
> To the freshest things now reigning and make stale
> The glistering of the present as my tale
> Now seems to it.   *Winter's Tale*, 4. Prol. 11–15.

The sense of the passage of time has itself become disordered: the same pleasant sense of

shock occurs in *The Tempest* in spite of its unities
(for instance, when Prospero "discovers" the
lovers at chess).

The difficulty of reconstructing Shakespeare's
productions is chiefly due to the crabbed stage
directions. There is little business that is not
implied in the dialogue; it is a matter of expand-
ing the hints, which are often ambiguous (e.g.
Polonius' "Take this from this", *Hamlet*, 2. 2,
l. 156). The author's stage directions were often
tentative, especially with regard to the number of
supers; they were expanded and particularised,
and in the case of undramatic authors, altered,
by the book-keeper, where they were not merely
indicative of business for a single actor.

The Bad Quartos often have particularly full
stage directions that suggest observations by a
spectator. Thus the Bad Quarto of *Romeo and
Juliet* has in 2. 6, "Enter Juliet rather fast and
embraceth Romeo", the 1599 Quarto merely
"Enter Juliet" (though Granville-Barker thinks
this is an alternate way of playing the scene,
where the sacramental nature of the marriage
is stressed by the restrained behaviour of the
characters). In 3. 1 the Bad Quarto has "Tibalt
under Romeo's arm thrusts Mercutio in, and

flies". The Good Quarto has merely "Away Tibald". In this case the situation can, of course, be reconstructed from the dialogue.

The Elizabethans naturally took their own stage for granted. References to "above", "the traverse", etc., are not expanded; technical terms such as "for" = "disguised as" ("Enter Rosalind for Ganimede", etc., *As You Like It*, 2. 4) were left in the Folio. The stage directions are often misplaced, too. An "entry" will come too soon merely because it means that the actor is to be ready "off". A premature exit may be explained, I think, by a reference to Kempe's remarks in *3 Parnassus* on the necessity of speaking on the way down stage, and not merely at the end of it. The player began his exit two or three lines before the end of his speech, because he had a long way to go before he was off. But exits are less carefully marked than entrances because they were not the book-keeper's business.

It is the book-keeper, we presume, who occasionally writes an actor's name instead of that of a character, as in *Much Ado about Nothing* Jack Wilson replaces Balthazar, and Kemp and Cowley, Dogberry and Verges. The prefixes often vary, too; they will be "Dogberry and Verges" or "Constable and Headborough" in different parts of the play. Perhaps this merely indicates a relaxing of attention on Shakespeare's part.

The book-keeper, too, noted what properties were to be prepared; these directions are always a few lines ahead of the appearance of the properties in the play. He arranged for people to be below to work the trap door, for the musicians to play music "off", but not apparently for the elaborate battle effects of the history plays.

A lack of knowledge of the structure of the Elizabethan stage has rarely caused anyone seriously to misunderstand Shakespeare's plays. The risk is greatest in the case of the later ones, where Shakespeare is depending more and more on its essential feature of neutrality. These plays are difficult to conceive of except in terms of Shakespeare's stage, and Dr Johnson, for instance, completely missed the point of the structure of *Antony and Cleopatra* and *Cymbeline* for this reason. He perceived the results but could not justify the causes. "This play keeps curiosity always busy, and the passions always interested....But the power of delighting is derived principally from the frequent changes of the scene...the events, of which the principal are described according to history, are produced without any art of connection or care of disposition."[1]

But most of Shakespeare's plays can be performed in some fashion on almost any stage. No one could read Racine or Ibsen without being aware of the peculiar local conditions for which they wrote; but it has been possible to ignore Shakespeare's, not because he did not himself consider them, but because there is so much more in his plays that they can be read or acted for one or two of their aspects only, just as anyone can play Hamlet fairly well. The few properties are the primitive features of any stage. Falstaff's or Polonius's "arras" only requires to be a hiding place: Lady Teazle's screen, Néron's ambush, or Rebecca West's curtain would serve equally well.

Such cruces as remain do not affect our appreciation of the plays. We do not know how Romeo leapt the orchard wall or how the soldiers

[1] Johnson: Note to *Antony and Cleopatra*.

[55]

surprised Cleopatra in her monument, nor would it add to the power of these scenes to learn.

The difficulties of exposition which the bare stage imposed were so easily surmounted by Shakespeare that it has needed a reconstruction of the stage to realise them. Characters have to explain much more: a great deal is provided for the modern audience by the setting (which indicates roughly time and place) and the programme (which blocks out the relationships of the dramatis personae). Shakespeare had to convey this indirectly, and for the most part it is delicately done. The openings of *Lear* and *As You Like It* are not typical. The necessity to dispose of dead bodies could produce such different effects as the end of *Lear* and the end of *Hamlet*.

After his early period, Shakespeare was not interested in stage mechanics for their own sake. Fantastic entries (like those in *Antonio and Mellida* where characters enter running or backwards), he replaced by delicate patterns of the kind to be found in *As You Like It*. He never showed any devotion to a particular piece of stage machinery, such as Chapman's taste for the trap door. Yet Shakespeare was conscious of delicate effects to be gained by grouping his actors, or by the presence of a silent figure like Cordelia or Virgilia. It is interesting to note how firmly he rejected some popular devices. He abandoned the induction (except for the *Taming of the Shrew* where it formed part of the old play) because it is difficult to relate it to the rest of the action; but he made use of the play within the play, a similar form, because it has ironic possibilities and allows for "shadow work" (*Love's Labour's Lost, Midsummer Night's Dream, Hamlet, The Tempest*). He seldom used the dumb show, either, though it survived late and had structural possibilities in the vivid presentation of matters relevant to the plot but not requiring much stress to be laid on them. (See *The Changeling*, 4. 1.) For such purposes it was much better than a conversation between First and Second Gentlemen; and if the rather too similar device of Hermione as the living statue had not been so close, it might possibly have been used for the recognition of Perdita by Leontes in *The Winter's Tale*.

Chapter V

THE TOPICAL ELEMENT IN
SHAKESPEARE

IT has long been the fashion to blame Shakespeare's audience for all that a change of
social standards makes unpalatable in his
plays, without much attempt to distinguish between the occasions when Shakespeare was in
agreement with his audience and those when he
was not. Only when something cuts across the
integrity of the play, changing its tone and movement, can it be ascribed to the influence of the
audience. The combats, the use of madness, and
the ghost in *Hamlet* were all popular tricks, but
we do not regard them as concessions. Nor
does much of the horseplay and bawdry that
distressed Dr Bridges seem to be supplied
reluctantly. The power of Shakespeare can be
measured by the ease with which he met a
definite local demand without degrading his
plays. During his maturity, one feels, he could
have made something out of any material, and
any of his plays might have turned out rather
differently yet equally well.

His contemporaries all regarded Shakespeare as a popular writer. The callow academics of *3 Parnassus* sneered at him for it. Webster classed him with Dekker and Heywood. Jonson poked fun at "York and Lancaster's long jars".

The difficulty of catering for the audience was increased by the fact that it was a very mixed one, and that it demanded much more from a play than a contemporary audience does. There are few plays on the boards now which aim at satisfying those whose interests lie in philosophic speculation, in rough-and-tumble comedy, in love songs, and in bawdry. But the problem was simplified by most of the audience wanting several of these things. The courtier was equally interested in the fencing displays and the wit combats; the groundling, though he preferred "inexplicable dumb shows and noise", would relish a Senecal phrase uttered in a pulpit manner—witness the oft quoted and probably apocryphal story of the good wife who had been as edified at a play as though she had attended a sermon, or the other chestnut (brought into *Hamlet*) of the effect of tragedies upon criminals.

The theatre represented several different kinds of amusement. It was a place to display fashions;

even the boxes of to-day cannot compete with the seats upon the stage. The fencing matches and "activities" were the Elizabethan equivalent of the football match, and the sensational stories and jingo patriotism of the cheaper press.

It has been noticed that Shakespeare rejected some of the devices most popular with his audience—the dumb show and conjuring (unless the witches in *Macbeth* are his attempt at it). He never attempted to write bourgeois tragedy nor, except for *The Merry Wives of Windsor*, bourgeois comedy.

There were also a number of things which he did to satisfy himself which must have passed unnoticed on the stage. Some plays were "cut"; *Hamlet* was too long to be acted, and the Folio version probably represents the usual theatrical text. Much of his dramatic irony, and the delicate hints of background or of the passage of time, must have been lost. None of his contemporaries asked for such close attention from their audience or offered them anything similar; and it is not likely that the audience would approach Shakespeare's plays in a different frame of mind from those of any other dramatist. Bradley urged that the imagination of an Elizabethan audience must have compensated for their love of horrors. But it is hardly possible that a blunted sensibility, only to be stirred by the horrors of *Titus*, could be united with a delicate and precise imagination. Nor is the audience's taste for poetry to be taken for granted. They probably enjoyed sententious common-places, and they would therefore respond to Hamlet's speeches exactly as to those of Marston's stern, stoical heroes. Their fondness for poetry is contradicted by the fact that they put up with so much bad poetry. A well-worn idea inviting moral assent, and declaimed in a stirring manner at the top of his voice by Burbage, is not "poetry".

Allusions to contemporary politics were a dangerous game which playwrights sometimes played. But Shakespeare does not seem to have practised it, though the discovery of this habit in his contemporaries set the diligent hunting, and they reduced the problems of *Hamlet* to those of the Scottish succession. There was some attempt to use *Richard II* by the conspirators in the Essex rebellion; the players were paid to stage it publicly. But Elizabeth neither fined nor imprisoned them, the deposition scene was in future cut out, and it was apparently recognised that the playwright had been innocent in his intentions and had merely been taken advantage of. Jonson, however, suffered unjustly from the Elizabethan habit of suspecting an allegorical interpretation to a play, and was imprisoned for writing "blasphemy and popery" in *Sejanus*. Shakespeare seems never actually to have been injured by the public taste for scandal. The Chamberlain's men were Elizabeth's favourite company, and it would have been most impolitic for them to risk disfavour by indiscretions of the kind for which Chapman and Jonson were imprisoned. When Shakespeare inserts a compliment to his sovereign, as in *Midsummer Night's Dream* or *Macbeth*, it is perfectly obvious; or a reference to Essex (Epilogue, *Henry V*) is made equally plain. It is not easy to see for whom the discoverers of more general significances thought that Shakespeare was planning them. If they were so very obscure, it is doubtful whether even an interested contemporary could grasp them; if he could not, it is to be assumed that Shakespeare was playing a kind of hide-and-seek to amuse himself, in the manner in which the Baconians imagine the Lord Chancellor to have embedded ciphers in the plays.

But the fashion for digging for allusions is clearly a disease of the incompetent pseudo-historian, unwilling to separate his own knowledge of facts from the plays.

Nor does Shakespeare seem to have taken any interest in the Poetomachia, with its more obvious personal allusions (the combat seems to have been played to the gallery rather than to have been a serious affair). Ben Jonson made capital out of his own reputation for bluffness: he introduces humorous portraits of himself into his inductions, cursing the players or beating the tiring man, which are rather too self-conscious for sincerity. His fondness for a picturesque rôle was evidently not confined to his stage performances as Hieronimo. Like Kent, as described by Cornwall, he knew the publicity value of a temperament:

> ... This is some fellow
> Who hath been praised for bluntness....

It is quite plainly indicated by the change of tone whenever Ben is attacking one of his enemies. Even without a knowledge of its stage history, it would be impossible to read *The Poetaster* without realising that Rufus and Demetrius Fannius were caricatures of particular persons. But if Shakespeare ever did administer the "purge" to Ben Jonson with which he has been credited, he has woven it so completely into the texture of his plays that the detection of it would serve no purpose beyond the satisfaction of curiosity. As it is only when they interfere with the straightforward movement of the play and clash with its dominant mood that it is profitable to consider his concessions to the audience, so it is only when they stand out from the body of the writing, when the particular intention has altered the quality of the style, that there is any point in recognising personal allusions. Shakespeare's one allusion to theatrical matters (the "little eyases" speech in *Hamlet*) proclaims itself for what it is: it seems probable that he would have made any other allusion equally unambiguous.

On the whole there is little that Shakespeare included in his plays against his will, though we cannot imagine this compromise as a conscious process, a decision to give the public what it wanted, and to produce a work of art into the bargain. He soon mastered the most potentially intractable element, the clowning. It is only possible to estimate the greatness of this achievement by comparing it with the helplessness of Heywood in *The Rape of Lucrece*, or Marston in *Antonio and Mellida*. Here Balurdo plays much the same part as the fool in *Lear*; he interrupts the tragic scenes with rhymes, and tries to defend the hero against the villain. (There are other parallels between *Antonio and Mellida* and *Lear*, e.g. the description of pretended suicide by falling from a cliff, a favourite device of Marston's; and the sub-plot which reverses the main plot, one being a son's revenge for his father, the other a father's revenge for his son. This type of sub-plot probably owed something to the play within the play, with its power of emphasising the main situation by reflecting it.)

The work of Thorndike and Stoll has been largely devoted to establishing the parallels between the course of Shakespeare's plays and that of contemporary fashion. His tragedies were written at a time when a revival of the taste for tragedy had been instituted, as his Romances suggest an attempt to compete with those of Beaumont and Fletcher.

This in itself is of little importance; a fashion for tragedy, or even for Revenge tragedy, implies so vague a demand that Shakespeare could have satisfied it in many ways. But as a matter of fact he borrowed in great detail, for *Hamlet* and *Lear* especially. Stoll has shown that there was an accepted code of behaviour for a Revenger, to which Hamlet conforms in the closest manner. It was his duty to come in wearing black, to utter certain Senecal commonplaces, to meditate on suicide, to simulate madness, to be in love with a lady who became really mad, to refuse to kill the villain because he would not send him to heaven.

Shakespeare was a great deal more circumscribed by his sources when he was dramatising Holinshead or North, but in this case his sources were already in dramatic form, and therefore he could reckon on his audience's familiarity with them. He could rely on their knowledge to limit their expectations, and so secure a greater concentration of interest. Minor matters could be slurred: valuable ambiguities, such as the position of Gertrude, were possible, which were essential to his play, without puzz-

ling the simpler minded, who would naturally
supply motives and statements from their knowledge of the old play.

It was inevitable that playwrights, composing
at the speed which most of the Elizabethans did,
should evolve certain conventions and build up
a stock of common ideas, phrases, dramatic
devices upon which anyone could freely draw.
The Revenge tragedy and the Beaumont and
Fletcher Romance were particularly popular
forms, and a whole series of incidents became
common property from which any dramatist
could quickly block out a play. But the lack of
any critical body, the fact that most playwrights
had not even any conscious critical principles,
meant that these conventions were used in a
purely pragmatical manner. They were never
recognised or openly accepted as implying a
limitation; they were utilised as conveniences.
The only limitation was in each writer's artistic
conscience. Dekker used the Revenger and all
his recognised accompaniments as part of a
realist bourgeois comedy, *The Honest Whore*,
Part 1; Marston employed him for his comedy
of *The Malcontent*. A character who had been
successful in a history would be put into a

comedy with no compunction. (Shakespeare served Falstaff in rather the same way in *The Merry Wives*: whether we feel personal indignation at his treatment or not, it is clear that he is not in the convention of bourgeois comedy.) Sequels were written for plays for which no sequel had been intended or was possible, if they had been a great success.

There is little to be gained by pointing out exactly how closely Shakespeare followed Kyd and Chettle and Marston; like Saint-Beuve's scientific criticism, it accounts for all of a work of art except the fact that it is a work of art. "There is a river in Monmouth and there is a river in Macedon...and there is salmons in both." But it is necessary to demonstrate how far in advance of his contemporaries Shakespeare was in his use of common form. He did not borrow pragmatically; he took over nothing that did not contribute to his final effects. There is no equivalent in the Canon for the gaoler's daughter in *The Two Noble Kinsmen*.

It is only a great artist who can afford to be a professional artist. The minor Elizabethans overwrote themselves; and consequently their early plays (Chapman's *Bussy*, Webster's *White Devil*

—for his collaborations can hardly be counted—
Beaumont and Fletcher's *Maid's Tragedy*) are
usually their best. The better of our minor
poets have usually been amateurs: even those
who wrote for a patron were in a better position
than nineteenth-century writers who wrote for
the public. Shakespeare seldom shows signs of
flagging, and he never takes refuge in a stock
effect.

These series of incidents, characters and
themes, conventions of character and plot create
a parallel to the verbal common forms of
Senecal sentence or proverbial saw. They were
more useful to the type of mind which, like
Tourneur's or Massinger's, preferred its material to be simplified, and relied on concentration. Shakespeare's complexity prevented his
using the more rigid conventions: they caused
some maladjustments in *Hamlet* and *Cymbeline*.
He preferred the more technical ones of patterned
speech or dialogue, or the use of expository
soliloquy and aside.

Richard III shows as much the influence of
Kyd's repetitions and parallelisms as of Marlowe. The stichomythia and repetition are used
only for scenes of lament or debate, not for

straightforward dialogue, i.e. they are employed only where a repetitive effect is relevant. Peele borrows them indiscriminately. In his later comedies Shakespeare uses rhyme to achieve the effects of pattern. Granville-Barker has noted[1] how in *Romeo and Juliet* the first meeting of the lovers is isolated and underlined by making them share a sonnet. The style of earlier tragedy is used for the play scenes in *Hamlet* to cut it off from the ordinary dialogue. Letters are usually written in a close antithetical style (Hamlet's epistle is not alone in this respect). As Shakespeare's command of language increased, his use of pattern became less obvious: compare the speech of Blanch of Spain (*King John*, 3. 1, l. 326) with that of Volumnia (*Coriolanus*, 5. 3, ll. 96–118). In both cases the aim is to exploit the mathematical possibilities of the situation, the number of permutations and combinations that may be gained from it. In the one case the speech is stiffly antithetical, in the other it is broken up by ejaculations, pauses and subordinate clauses.

There are many trivial mechanical devices that Shakespeare uses, particularly in his his-

[1] *Prefaces to Shakespeare*, Second Series.

tories and comedies. It was, for instance, a
source of pleasure to his audience to be reminded
in the play of the conditions of the playhouse.
Dramatic spectacle was a novelty, and they liked
their own position as spectators to be dramatised.
The characters would sometimes make equi-
vocal remarks or refer to themselves in their
capacity as actors. Thus at the end of *Antonio's
Revenge*, Act 1, Pandulpho bids, "Strike loud
music to this dreadful act", where "act" =
"crime", but also act-interval: it was "the
music for the act" for which he was calling. When
in *Julius Caesar* (3. 1, l. 111) Cassius says:

> ...How many ages hence
> Shall this our lofty scene be acted o'er
> In states unborn and accents yet unknown,

the audience would recognise with something of
the pleasure to be gained from a pun that they
were present at one of these foretold occasions.
Sometimes a pun was actually used: "Hung be
the heavens with black, yield day to night",
applied, as Bedford spoke it, to the sky; as the
actor spoke it, to the heavens of the theatre,
which were hung with black for tragedies. The
fun of the page disguise for heroines lay in the
fact that they really were boys; and Rosalind in

[71]

the Epilogue to *As You Like It* makes open play on this, "I would kiss as many of you as had beards that pleased me". The inductions of Ben Jonson and Marston were probably popular for a similar reason, and in the play within the play the audience saw themselves reflected in the dignified stage spectators. It was almost as though they were taking part in the play, as Beaumont and Fletcher made their Grocer's apprentice do.

The history plays are Shakespeare's only consistent attempts at a personal convention. Here he is less interested in his people as individuals: and the action is always of national rather than personal importance (which is perhaps the justification of Prince Hal). The series seems to aim at a certain completeness and continuity; this in itself is a modification of the history play peculiar to Shakespeare.

The only kind of unity which he could impose was by stressing the repetition of situations, the sense of a recurrent pattern. However shapeless a play may be, it is always carefully linked to its predecessor and successor. Gloucester is developed at the end of *3 Henry VI*, Prince Hal at the end of *Richard II*, and the wars and Catherine of France are promised us at the end of

2 *Henry IV*. The chief device is the use of omens or prophecies, usually of an ambiguous kind, and of the sense of satisfied expectancy at seeing their unexpected fulfilment. Thus in *Richard III* Anne and Buckingham unwittingly curse themselves, and afterwards recall that the curse is now fulfilled. Rivers, Vaughan and Grey recall Margaret's curse on their way to execution. The laments sum up the misfortunes of both houses. There is the riddling prophecy about "G", and the prediction that Richard shall not live long after he sees Rougemont. In 2 *Henry IV* the prophecy that the king is to die in Jerusalem receives an unlooked-for fulfilment; there is a prophecy about John's death, and the giving up of his crown; and in 2 *Henry VI* the riddle that Suffolk is to die by water is fulfilled by a dreadful pun. In *Richard II* (4. 1) the Bishop of Carlisle prophesies the whole course of the Wars of the Roses; John of Gaunt foresees the future before his death; Henry VI forecasts the future of Richmond, and veiled references to Elizabeth are common. There are also retrospective speeches such as those in 2 *Henry IV* (4. 1, l. 113 and 1. 2, l. 100) which look back to *Richard II* (1. 3 and 5. 2 respectively).

[73]

The history plays can only be shaped by some such drastic and mechanic means; there is too much stubborn fact to permit of free handling. The recital of genealogical tables evidently pleased the people, for they occur frequently; and the plays are full of supers, that many nobles with familiar and sounding titles may be introduced. Sometimes the pattern is a stage one: "Enter a father who has killed his son, and a son who has killed his father", or the processional entries of Oxford, Somerset and Montague in *3 Henry VI* (5.1). The different kings are pivotal figures for the contrasts of the plays. In some things they are alike: they all have soliloquies on the hardships of a crown and the happiness of peasants. The attitude to England is constant also. When in *3 Henry VI* (4.1, l. 43) we read—

Let us be backed with God and with the seas
Which God hath given for force impregnable,

or in *John* (2.1, l. 22):

...that pale, that white faced shore
Whose foot spurns back the ocean's warring tides
And coops from other lands her islanders,

—it is not necessary to turn up the speech of John of Gaunt.

[74]

This mechanical use of repetition prepared Shakespeare for the subtler repetitions of imagery and phrase that are the very texture of his tragedies. He might have scoffed at their obviousness later, but they were excellent training.

These devices of construction are similar to the verbal borrowings in their effects. They give the dramatist a kind of bony framework on which to build. The Senecal tradition—in so far as there was a Senecal tradition behind Elizabethan tragedy—was passed on by means of these common phrases, which were borrowed so frequently that it becomes futile to talk of borrowing. "Per scelera semper sceleribus tutum est iter" (*Ag.* 115) was perhaps the most hard-worked tag. It occurs in *The Spanish Tragedy, The Misfortunes of Arthur, Macbeth, Richard III, Cataline, The White Devil, The Duke of Milan*; and in *The Malcontent*, where it is quoted much as "Yes we have no bananas" might be, "Pooh! Per scelera semper sceleribus tutum est iter". "Curae laeves loquantur, ingentes stupeant" was almost as popular. It appears in *Sir T. Wyatt, Sir T. More, Revenger's Tragedy, White Devil, The Widow's Tears, Macbeth* and *The Broken Heart*. These phrases belong to the simplified characters and stereotyped plot of the Revenge tragedy; they are part of its machinery, but how far they are assimilated and how far merely adopted can be tested by the delicacy and force with which they are restated. The last tag appears in *Macbeth* as:

> ...The griefs which *dare not speak*
> *Whisper* the o'erfraught heart, and bid it break.

The metaphor has completely modified the old worn phrase, with its suggestion of terrified restraint, harrowing with fear and wonder. When the Elizabethans borrowed it was nearly always verbally; they took the words as well as the idea, which makes their thefts peculiarly easy to track. But this very literalness meant that a certain pressure was brought to bear upon the phrase and that it became more completely fused with its context. Chapman borrowed from Erasmus, Webster from Sidney, and Jonson from all sorts of places, but the convolutions of Chapman, the staccato epigrams of Webster, and the careful *mots justes* of Jonson do not suggest illegitimate borrowing to an ordinary reader; yet in the *White Devil* there are twenty-four phrases which Webster has copied from his notebook, and twenty-three which he has repeated from his own earlier plays, or was to repeat in later plays.

Shakespeare did not borrow very frequently except from his immediate source; his right happy and copious industry exempted him. Where he did (as in the passage from Florio's Montaigne in *The Tempest*) he, too, was quite literal. The habit of working closely from sources probably affected the Elizabethans. Those who were actors must also have known many plays by heart, and there is his own testimony to the prodigious nature of Jonson's memory.

It has been urged that though this kind of reference "may have provided a groundwork, and there is a natural curiosity in seeing what this was, there cannot be anything seriously gained by observing Shakespeare's little shifts and contrivances". It seems, on the contrary, that everything is to be gained by realising how completely he fitted them into his plays, and that with the minimum of alteration and distortion of material. Much more of his work than is imagined has this topical and local implication; for if Shakespeare had not a single tradition to work in, he had the débris and fragments of many traditions, literary and dramatic.

Chapter VI

THE QUESTION OF
CHARACTERISATION

IT seems clear that Shakespeare's contemporaries appreciated him chiefly because of individual characters in the plays. Falstaff was the most famous, condemned to the futility of "a second appearance" at the request, tradition says, of Queen Elizabeth. Leonard Digges witnesses to the extreme popularity of Benedick and Beatrice and of Malvolio, "that cross-gartered Gull". The writers of the late seventeenth and early eighteenth centuries appreciated the characters as easily recognisable types; it was because Iago departed from the typical behaviour of a stage soldier that Rymer objected to him, and Johnson felt it necessary to apologise for Menenius in the double character of statesman and buffoon. The actors moved the characters from one play to another to provide more "fat" parts in one production; Benedick and Beatrice, for instance, were imported into *Measure for Measure* to cheer it up as much as possible. The nineteenth century rejected the stage and looked on the characters as responsible individuals, which did some of them (Prince Hal or Bertram of Roussillon) as much violence as Rymer had done Iago. The dramatis personae were detached from their play and their background; the naïve demanded "more" like Queen Elizabeth; and Mary Cowden Clarke produced, not in isolation, *The Girlhood of Shakespeare's Heroines*.

This emphasis on the characters was quite healthy while it remained an interest in defining and recognising the types as "just representations of general Nature". Johnson's best piece of work on Shakespeare is his character of Polonius. But when it became a question of individuals, and the Romantics had settled down to pick the bones and pluck out the heart of Hamlet's mystery, the interest was bound to connect itself with analysis of behaviour and motivation. The characters became real, all-round, solid human beings, judged by the standards, including the moral ones, of ordinary life. (Though the moral judgment is relevant to literature, it can hardly be applied to single characters in isolation, or even to the dramatist's implicit judgment of these fragmentary parts of his work.)

Judgment by characterisation, and therefore

by story as distinct from plot, led to a serious distortion of some of Shakespeare's plays. *The Tempest* could be no more than a charming phantasy, or a profound allegory; *A Midsummer Night's Dream* had not even the alternative. Moreover, this method of treating a play implies that it is no more than the sum of its parts; that the mere juxtaposition, as distinct from contrast or interaction, of characters may not in itself contribute to the total effect. A case in point is *Twelfth Night*, where the delicately satiric point of view provides a unity of tone, and explains how, in spite of the apparent detachment of the Malvolio group, they could not be replaced by a Touchstone-Audrey combination (who are farcical rather than satiric) without upsetting the balance of the play.

The nineteenth-century critic approached the characters as he did the dramatists; as friends, to be loved or quarrelled with. Lamb admired Heywood for his English gentlemen and his English gentlemen for qualities which he found admirable in Wordsworth. The view persisted. "Other friends we have of Shakespeare's giving whom we love deeply and well, if hardly with such love as could weep for them all the tears of the body, and all the blood of the heart: but there is none we love like Othello."[1] Even Dr Bradley cannot keep his personal feelings under control. When Lear kneels to pray in the storm, he exclaims: "This is one of the things that make us ready to *worship* Shakespeare".

Hamlet is the stock example of this misplaced affection. Ophelia is not the only inoffensive innocent driven to madness by his wayward charm. His history has been explored from his earliest childhood; "hidden motives and un-revealed ideas" have been exploited to the full. He has been explained in terms of his relationship to other single characters—Ophelia, his mother, or Claudius; his medical history has been studied, though it has never yielded quite such satisfactory results as the murder of Desdemona.[2]

The interest in character made certain plays inexplicable. The bitter comedies had to be distorted or ignored. *All's Well* becomes "one of the most pleasing of our author's comedies", with Bertram as a brusquer Fitzwilliam D'Arcy, or later (when the play was decided to be Shavian satire) a despicable cur. Some of the

[1] Swinburne, *Studies in Shakespeare*.
[2] See Variorum, *Othello*, pp. 302–307.

[81]

greatest plays, *Lear* and *Antony and Cleopatra*, for example, cannot be profitably considered by an analysis of individual dramatis personae, for though convincing as "characters" in the play, they are not convincing as persons, because they are not separable from the play as a whole.

Furthermore, far too much stress was laid on minor characters who are hardly ever separable from their functions in the plot. For Victor Hugo, *Lear* was the tragedy of Cordelia, who is definitely a minor figure. The women were particularly over-emphasised. Possibly her conformity to the domestic ideal accounts for the extraordinary idolatry of Imogen.

But Shakespeare's characters are not only the personal friends of nineteenth-century critics; they offer them dramatic scope. Coleridge made Hamlet in his own image and most of the lesser criticism involved no more than mental productions of the plays, the critic outdoing even the Elizabethan actor by doubling all the parts. This shows how far removed from the stage the plays had become, when each person's private acting version was offered as a serious commentary.

It was only a step farther to put Shakespeare behind his puppets, and to arrive at the Frank

Harris method of interpretation. This has a certain limiting effect, since Shakespeare's dramatic capabilities are confined to the rôle of the hero. (Though I do not see why he should not play a very effective Desdemona. Her adjective "gentle" is notoriously his: the Moor would be an easy avatar for the Dark Lady and Iago would probably be a separate dramatisation of her baser self, ruining her own better nature (Othello) and Mr W. H. (Cassio), the fair man who had "gone a wooing" for his friend. W. H.'s relations with Desdemona (Shakespeare) are blackened, and his early platonic relationship with herself is likewise shattered.)

The personal interpretation has never been taken very seriously; but the treatment of the characters as living beings died hard. Bradley's *Shakespearean Tragedy*, with its appendices on Lady Macbeth's children and similar subjects, was the brilliant *reductio ad absurdum* of the system; but such was its influence that for some years it prevented the percolation of the researches on stage conditions into appreciative criticism. Even studies of the dramatist, such as that of Brander Matthews, are thinly disguised gossip about the private lives of the dramatis

[83] 6-2

personae; Helen of Narbon is still reproved for her conversation on virginity, "impossible to a modest minded girl".[1] The individual studies of *Hamlet* and *Othello* by Stoll, and Schücking's *Die Charakterprobleme bei Shakespeare*, were the first serious attacks upon orthodoxy.

Shakespeare was found to fall short in two respects of realistic treatment of his characters. He made them behave inconsistently, and motivated them inadequately. Sometimes he merely neglected to supply a motive; the critics were ready enough to do this for him, but they could not always fit it to the text. Coleridge, for instance, would have inserted a clause in the Oracle's message in *The Winter's Tale*, which, by obliging Hermione to live concealed until Perdita was found, would have relieved her from a possible charge of hard-heartedness.

But Shakespeare also neglected motivation when it was already supplied in his sources. King Leir had a perfectly watertight reason for his demand for a public declaration of affection. Isabella's original had a reason for begging the life of the wicked deputy. As it is there is not a single play of Shakespeare's where the motiva-

[1] Brander Matthews, *Shakespeare the Dramatist*.

tion for every character is quite sufficient, except in those comedies where he assumes arbitrary conventions of love at first sight, sudden repentance, and miraculous coincidence. The most glaring example of his indifference to motivation is Coriolanus, whose change of party in the middle of the play (the event upon which the catastrophe directly depends) is absolutely unprepared and unexplained. Antonio, in *The Merchant of Venice*, is a less intractable person, but only to be explained by "sentiments not avowed".

Inadequate motivation may pass over into inconsistency. Leontes might be described by either label. The simplest cases of inconsistency occur when a character makes a speech "out of character", such as Prince Hal's opening soliloquy—"I know you all". A single speech may be "out of character" in a different way, however, by its manner as well as its matter. Mercutio on Queen Mab or Polonius' advice to Laertes are the usual examples of this. They are irrelevant and unsuitable, but not unnatural; they have the detachable quality of an operatic aria.

There are two parallel types of inconsistency in action. The behaviour of Isabella in *Measure for Measure*, of Claudio in *Much Ado*, simply contradicts their professions and their friends' views of them, as Hal's speech does. Henry V is turned into a country bumpkin in the final scene of the play, to give his wooing the right note of heartiness and democratic sentimentality, though hitherto he had been an adroit and polished diplomat. But the behaviour of Posthumus or Othello is contradictory in a different way. The Othello of the first act is no more than a magnificent study in poise, judgment and *savoir faire*. "Put up your bright swords, for the dew will rust them!" It is impossible logically that he should ever become horn-mad: neither predisposition to jealousy, racial differences, nor the "devilish" skill of Iago is adequate to explain his taking the word of a subordinate against his wife and his best friend.[1] He is as unjustified as Posthumus, for whom "weakling" is the usual epithet, or as Imogen (who is deceived more easily than either of them, but who is always justified: it is amusing to see Granville-Barker gobbling up all the bait of excuses and evasions which Shakespeare has laid down about this passage).

[1] Stoll has treated this question at great length.

Also, there are certain characters who seem altogether inconsistent: Hamlet, Falstaff, Cleopatra. Like the sacred griffin in the *Purgatorio* they seem to have two natures, and we can see them reflected in Shakespeare "or con uni, or con altri reggimenti". This "inconsistency" is precisely the cause of their greatness; but it has puzzled the critics, and, unwilling to bear the ills they have, they have flown to others.

Schücking tackles the character problem through the traces of a more primitive technique surviving in Shakespeare. In the Miracle plays the various personages used a narrative method of exposition. They would convey information directly to the audience, not only of their circumstances—

> I am a lord that mickle is of might,
> Prince of all Jewry, Sir Pilate I hight,[1]

—but of their feelings, motives and intentions. Nothing was obliquely stated or left to be inferred by the audience.

The soliloquy was the particular province for this direct information. It had almost the same

[1] *Wakefield Miracle Play of the Crucifixion.*

objective character as the prologue or epilogue. The Elizabethan stage particularly encouraged this kind of soliloquy. The actor was well down on the fore-stage, surrounded on three sides by the audience. He was probably so well known to them that it was difficult to remember that he was acting a part. (A regular attendance at a repertory theatre soon proves the effort necessary to sink a knowledge of an actor in his part, especially if he is on the stage alone and unengaged in any particular business.) The soliloquy puzzled the nineteenth century: delivered from a picture stage, it is usually ridiculous. The undramatic nature of the soliloquy is the basis of most of Schücking's arguments, and his attitude is largely dependent on a fuller grasp of the principles of Elizabethan staging.

The aside is of course a parallel form to the soliloquy. It may be merely explanatory, like Desdemona's

> I am not merry, but I do beguile
> The thing I am by seeming otherwise,

or Othello's "O hardness to dissemble". It may be expository, and therefore long and meditative (Cornelius's in *Cymbeline*, 1. 4, l. 33, is one of the

most amusingly naïve). The ironic punning
aside ("A little more than kin, and less than
kind") is nearer to stichomythia and the verbal
patterns of Kydian tragedy.

Schücking's theories dismiss a great many of
the misunderstandings which had arisen through
the confusion of the dramatis personae with real
people. He begins with "Self-characterisation":
Hamlet and Falstaff dissect themselves; Cordelia, Troilus and Caesar praise themselves in a
manner which, if we allow the statement to be
made "in character", suggests boastfulness.
Villains are unnaturally sure of their own
wickedness, and of the goodness of the heroes:
Oliver, Edmund, Iago and Cassius illustrate
this. There are several border-line cases. Laertes,
however, is assumed to be correct in his description of Hamlet's attitude to Ophelia, though
Lady Macbeth is not altogether right about the
character of her husband. Schücking also deals
with verbal contradictions, such as the question
of Lady Macbeth's children, the reality of her
fainting, and the correct account of Ophelia's
death. (That of the Queen contradicts the
Clown's; though Schücking does not observe
that the Queen's account is in any case impos-

sible, because if Ophelia's death could be described in such detail—

> ...Her clothes spread wide,
> And mermaid-like awhile they bore her up,
> What time she chanted fragments of old tunes...

—it must have been seen by someone near enough to have rescued her.)

Finally, he discusses the characters of Hamlet and of Cleopatra, and attempts to explain them.

Schücking's difficulties arise from his extreme literal-mindedness. When Iago talks of Othello remaining calm while the cannon

> ...from his very arm
> Puffed his own brother,

Schücking assumes that we have a parallel to Lady Macbeth's children, and declares himself puzzled, "having thought of Othello as a friendless man". Friar Lawrence is accused of impropriety in saying, "Affliction is enamoured of thy parts", and Lady Capulet in making a reference to marginal glosses, since the Friar should have no experience of the tender passion, or the Lady of commentaries. If metaphors are to be strictly limited to personal experience in this manner, the English language is in an even more deplorable state than has been realized.

A difficulty is created where none has been suspected. Bottom's remarks to the fairy attendants are considered too witty to be in character, though they are not above the level of a cockney cab-driver's repartee. No character is allowed a mixed motive or a complex interpretation. Hence the failure to deal with Cleopatra: either she is a courtesan, and shameless, or she is a devoted lover, and respectable (the Moral Judgment intervenes here, of course). Macbeth is decided to be simply a vicious weakling, for a reason all too clear, "he is the very opposite of a heroic character of ancient *Northern* strength and endurance". The whole play is distorted in consequence; "This Duncan hath borne his faculties so meek", becomes mere description of hero by villain, as mechanical a tribute as Oliver's to Orlando. And because Macbeth, when Banquo questions him on his "rapt" behaviour in 1. 3, does not explain that it is caused by meditations on regicide, he is "like all weak characters, a liar". Such passages as 1. 7, ll. 31 ff. (and presumably also "Duncan is in his grave", and "My way of life") are quite arbitrarily declared to be "mere transitory emotions...and not really firm convictions". Finally, Lady Macbeth, though she sums up Macbeth's behaviour correctly in 1. 5, does not give the right reasons for it, because here Shakespeare forgets for a moment every rule of the Objective Truth in Soliloquy, and makes a miscalculation.

The handling of Shylock is equally over-simplified. It is only by ignoring the evidence that he can be made into a plain out-and-out villain, as Schücking attempts to do. It has been felt, from Rowe onwards, that he claims our sympathy in a limited way. But no one has observed that the Elizabethans could give their sympathy in a less niggardly manner than we, and not merely where it could be reinforced by a moral identification with the character. The real parallel to Shylock is not Barabbas, but Volpone; it is possible to enter fully and sympathetically into Volpone's delight in his gold, while dissociating oneself from his attitude towards his dupes. I do not think the comparison is invalidated by the fact that Volpone's feelings are æsthetic and therefore largely impersonal, while Shylock's are racial and personal.

The Elizabethans liked the villain-hero, the ambiguous character who excited paradoxical feelings, and with whom a limited identification was possible.[1] Hence the absurdity of approaching Vindice as a "fallen angel", or a "blasted splendour"[2]; a Miltonic Satan to whom a single mixed response is given. His two sides must be seen separately, as Marston's Antonio saw Julio's two natures, and loved him while he carved him up, or as Othello kissed Desdemona ere he killed her.

> ...O thou weed
> That art so lovely fair, and smell'st so sweet.

The two views are held simultaneously and yet quite separately in his mind with a terrifying clearness, and yet they are irreconcilable. It is this which makes their peculiar intensity; it deepens them both, like the juxtaposition of complementary colours. Hamlet has a rather similar feeling about his mother:

> ...Sense sure you have,
> Else could you not have motion.   (3. 1, l. 71.)

Dissociation is at its simplest and strongest in Spenser: the Bower of Bliss is described and

[1] As in *Richard III, White Devil, Malcontent, Spanish Tragedy, The Jew of Malta, Faustus, Revenger's Tragedy, Macbeth.*

[2] Allardyce Nicoll, Preface to *Tourneur's Works.*

[93]

demolished with equal gusto; the gusto, in fact, largely depends on this reconciliation of opposites.

Schücking is clearly pleased with the "scientific" nature of his approach. He would reduce Shakespeare's method to a formula. He is constantly obliged to make exceptions to his own rules, e.g. Lady Macbeth's soliloquy, mentioned above; Iago's opening speeches—he insists especially that characters must tell the truth at the opening—which contain a particularly calumnious attack on Othello; Cassius on Caesar's weakness. We are told that Cassius is so envious that no one could take him seriously; but this applies even more to the blacker villains, Oliver, Iago and Edmund, who pay tribute to the heroes. Laertes' opening speech on Hamlet is taken to be correct, but it is not mentioned whether this means that his explanation of the Prince's attentions as an attempt at seduction is also to be accepted.

Schücking is helpful enough in destroying minor difficulties of "A fellow almost damned in a fair wife" kind.[1] His interpretations of the

---

[1] A glance at the Variorum (*Othello*, 1. 1, l. 21) is enlightening.

chief characters are, however, too "scientific"
and simpliste. He does not distinguish sufficiently between Shakespeare's occasional lapses
into a primitive technique, and his deliberate use
of a convention, in such parts of a play as he was
not concerned to develop. Thus in *Much Ado* he
boldly takes a stock villain and creates a compli-
cation by artificial means. An we will take it, so;
an we will not, so. Portia's news of the safety of
Antonio's ships—

> You shall not know by what strange accident
> I chanced on this letter...   (5. 1, l. 278)

—is referred to by the editors of the Cambridge
New Shakespeare as "masterly impudence".
But here Shakespeare was not interested in
motivation, and made no attempt to disguise it.
Webster throws in a superficial explanation of
Ferdinand's cruelty to the Duchess of Malfi:

>   ...I hoped to get
> An infinite mass of treasure by her death.

There is clearly no question of its sufficiency as a
motive; it is there to be accepted if anyone feels
in need of a motive; if not, it can be ignored.

This kind of "impudence" seems to me
perfectly conscious. I cannot believe that when

Shakespeare wrote Prince Hal's opening soliloquy, he did not know that he was doing
something different from writing the opening
soliloquy of *Richard III*. Richard is a consistently simplified character: he has the vigour and
resilience of a circumscribed type, like Volpone
or Barabbas. Hal is partly an individual and
partly an automaton. "I am determined to be a
villain" does not clash with the wooing of Anne
or Elizabeth—for these, too, are artificial—as "I
know you all" does with the scenes in the Boar's
Head. In *Henry IV*, in *Much Ado*, Shakespeare
was using his own earlier method without
modification, after he had outgrown it. By the
time he was writing Othello's soliloquies, he
had reached equilibrium. Othello sees himself
in a dramatic light, but he retains his individual
tone and accent while doing so.

Stoll's point of view is similar to Schücking's,
but, like Thorndike, he uses chiefly the comparative method. *Hamlet* is examined in terms of
The Spanish Tragedy, of Chettle's *Hoffman*, and of
Antonio's Revenge. In his studies of *Hamlet* and
Othello he has pointed out that no rational
explanation for the behaviour of the characters
can be devised. His explanation is that in spite

of the completely illogical nature of the story, the characters are "real" because they retain a personal and individual tone. His paper on "The Comic Method" develops this theory. Shakespeare is not concerned to weave a pattern of comic intrigue; the comedy is in the conception of the characters, and the incidents only serve to show it up. The characters can be thought of apart from the particular situations in which they appear, as the characters of Molière, for instance, can not.

Stoll protests that in trying to judge Shakespeare's characters by psychological standards we are only repeating the mistake of the Renaissance in reading moral allegories into all the classics. "We should be content with the poet and dramatist." In place of psychology, Shakespeare had "an infinite tact, the artist's delicate flexible touch". Though Othello cannot be explained logically, his tone and accent remain the same; the "antres vast, and deserts idle" fit in well enough with the images of the Sybil in her prophetic fury, or the Pontic sea. In imagery, sentiment, movement, Othello remains the same, and if it were possible for the hero of Act 1 to be reduced to the helpless madman of

Act 4, this is the voice in which he would speak. As Dr Johnson says: "He shows us human nature, not only as it acts in real exigencies, but as it would be found in trials to which it cannot be exposed".

In recognising the difference between the depiction and the motivation of character, Stoll has done an immense service to Shakespearean criticism. It was this "individual tone and accent" which enchanted the eighteenth century as being so close to nature, while the conventional stage motivation reassured them as to the propriety of the type. (Dr Johnson on Autolycus illustrates this particularly well.) But in the development of a character Shakespeare was as a rule not interested. None of the other Elizabethans, except possibly Middleton in *The Changeling*, ever showed a character otherwise than as static and fixed. The villains remained villains (until the last act if it were a comedy) and the heroes had no lapses from heroism.

Macbeth is usually cited as an exception. But Shakespeare does not explain his development, and that of Lady Macbeth is even more obscure, while both are complicated by the supernatural element. The development is shown through imagery and the particular use of words, through poetry; it could not be paraphrased in terms of psychology or in prose at all. Stoll notes the subtle movement in *Othello*, shown by the five successive encounters of Othello and Desdemona, after his first suspicions have been aroused. This again is not a matter to be mapped on a psychological chart; it is not a construction of the mere intelligence.

In some respects (on the question of Shylock or Falstaff for instance, or in his early papers on the villain) Stoll judges as narrowly as Schücking. His New England conscience condemns Shylock, and Falstaff is no more than a butt. He is also too inclined to insist that Shakespeare could not modify traditional material, e.g. Hamlet must mean the literal truth when he declares that he will not kill his uncle only to send him to heaven. In spite of Nash's *Unfortunate Traveller's* story, and all the other sources for this device, I cannot but think that if it is a literal truth it is being used in a rather Jesuitical manner.

The comparative method, if carried to extremes, obscures the issues rather as Sainte-Beuve's studies of "L'homme, le milieu, et le

[99]

moment" did: they explain everything except why Pierre Corneille was not exactly like his brother Thomas. This over-emphasis is partly due to the fact that a minority must be belligerent, and Stoll is putting his case to sceptics. But it makes the judicious inclined to view him, as M. Émile Legouis evidently does,[1] with one auspicious and one drooping eye.

It is now generally conceded that Shakespeare was not exclusively interested in his characters (and we have Aristotle's sanction for the pre-eminence of the plot). I think a distinction should be drawn between his heroic and his comic characters. The Elizabethans, unlike Racine, but like Corneille, held the royalist view of character. Their heroes were usually reigning monarchs or at the least petty princes, and further they were Italians, Asiatics or Romans, whose feelings were not as those of ordinary men. Therefore a "sight too pitiful in the meanest wretch" becomes "past speaking of in a king". Their affections are "higher than ours", and that they "stoop with like wing" is a matter

[1] *La Réaction contre la critique Romantique de Shakespeare* (Essays and Studies of the English Association, 1928).

sufficiently odd to be pointed out. It is only
in the moments of their greatest pain that they
become human; this indicates the height from
which they have fallen:

> No more, but e'en a woman and commanded
> By the same passion as the maid that milks
> And does the meanest chares.

> Every puny whipster gets my sword.

> ...I melt and am not
> Of stronger earth than others.

Cleopatra, Coriolanus and Othello soar again
before their deaths.

The villain and the hero are sometimes in
rather a special position. Granville-Barker has
noted that Lear has to act the storm,[1] but at this
point he has also to act the whole tragedy.
Consequently he is unnaturally "fixed", ex-
hibited as it were for the whole of Act 3, dis-
playing his agony detachedly and impersonally
in his long soliloquies. The Duchess of Malfi in
the whole of Act 4 sits in a similar state, as
though she were posing for a portrait,

> Like patience on a monument
> Smiling at grief,

[1] *Prefaces to Shakespeare*, 2nd Series.

with a fixed tragic mask like that of the Greeks.
(The Scene of Suffering occurs to the mind as
the Greek equivalent for this detached exhibi-
tion: and in particular the speeches of Prometheus in *Prometheus Bound*.)

The villain, too, must exhibit the tragedy, he
must state the tragic situation: the issue is put,
and not merely implied. Therefore he too is
unnaturally detached, analytic of his own villainy
and the hero's virtue. The conscienceless Machia-
vellian—the Italian devil with no inside—was
very useful for this. Iago's soliloquies may be
compared with the speech of Monsieur in
Bussy D'Ambois, 5. 2. The situation is stated and
completely stated, because it is in the total
situation rather than in the wrigglings of individual emotion that the tragedy lies.

Shakespeare's difficulty lies in the fact that
he was interested in complete human beings, and
his power over words allowed him to produce
characters which seem complete. Yet they are
usually a stage type at the same time: Falstaff is
the Braggart Soldier; that is the skeleton, completely enveloped in an individuality as solid as
his own corporal being. Yet at any moment he
may be called upon to play his small stage rôle,

for which he has grown out of all compass. The lesser dramatists, working inside the types, achieved their effects by different means, by frankly unreal figures (except Webster, who encountered the same difficulties as Shakespeare, but had less structural ability, and so failed to camouflage his difficulties).

Mrs Woolf's plea against Ford's Anabella,[1] and by implication against most Elizabethan dramatic characters, is that we do not "know" her; too much happens to her in the play for us to see its effect upon her. Anabella is compared with Anna Karenina. But Ford was not making an attempt to draw a person, as Tolstoi was; to expect it is to demand a novel of a dramatist (a not inexplicable demand from Mrs Woolf). Anabella is only part of the patterned order of the play; a conventional figure, not a human being. It is not easy to see why "real" characters should be demanded in poetry or in fiction; it seems merely a variation of photographic realism.

The comic characters are not very different. They are to be as "natural", as near to vulgar humanity as possible, to throw the hero up in relief; and therefore their absurdity is carried

[1] Notes on an Elizabethan play—*The Common Reader*.

beyond all human possibility. Shallow and Dogberry and Bottom are more monstrous fools than Nature ever produced. Though the conventions are no longer so visible, they are present. And the comic figures are generally more dependent on their fellows; they produce a collective effect. Bottom requires Quince and Starveling, Dogberry Verges, Costard the other Worthies. Falstaff is an exception; he is not so closely dependent on his retinue, and partakes more of the character of the hero.

Chapter VII

SHAKESPEARE AND THE
"PROFESSION"

THOUGH the knowledge of Elizabethan
stage conditions is now sufficient to give
an idea of how Shakespeare's plays should
be presented, Elizabethan acting is not familiar
enough to make it easy to decide how he should
be played. Any attempts to discuss the question
has usually stopped short at a recital of the
evidence to show that Kempe played Peter in
Romeo and Juliet and Dogberry in *Much Ado*;
that the company possessed a tall thin actor
(Armado, Aguecheek, etc.) and two boys, one
of whom was short and dark, and played Her-
mia, Celia and perhaps Maria in *Twelfth Night*,
the other taking Helena, Rosalind, and Viola;
that Shakespeare himself perhaps played the
Ghost in *Hamlet* and Adam in *As You Like It*.

There is little that can be directly inferred
from the plays about the style of acting at the
Globe. There are many incidental references to
players, some of which, like that on the feeling

of a poor actor entering after a well-graced one,[1]
or of the nervous actor who forgets his part,[2]
sound like personal reminiscences. The more
detached references usually ridicule the actor.
Troilus speaks of

> ...a strutting player, whose conceit
> Lies in his hamstring, and does think it rich
> To hear the wooden dialogue and sound
> Twixt his stretched footing and the scaffolding,
>
> (1. 3, l. 153)

and Buckingham will

> ...counterfeit the deep tragedian,
> Start and look pale at wagging of a straw.

Macbeth speaks of the poor player that "struts
and frets his hour upon the stage". Titus
Andronicus asks, when he is mutilated,

> ...how can I grace my speech
> Wanting a hand to give it action?

which suggests a very conventional gesture
(compare the reference to "the pitiful action of
old Titus, with his one arm"). There are very
few passages which speak well of the actor, and
those, like that of Brutus (*Julius Caesar*, 2. 1, l.
225), are not likely to be personal.

[1] *Richard II*, 5. 2, l. 23.
[2] Sonnet 23.

It is known that Shakespeare's company was not so much given to ranting as Henslowe's, which had Alleyn to play anything in Ercles' vein. It has been suggested that Falstaff's parody of King Cambyses, and Pistol's mouthings (*1 Henry IV*, 2. 4, l. 436, *2 Henry IV*, 5. 3) are gibes at the rival players; the lines in the latter passages are all taken from plays in their repertory, and they had just produced *Sir John Oldcastle* as a rival attraction to *Henry IV*.

It is to be inferred that Shakespeare did not like highly coloured acting. In this he was in the company of Ben Jonson, who repudiated "scenical strutting and furious vociferation" as well as those stage effects of "drummers making thunder in the tiring house, and twelve penny hirelings artificial lightening in the heavens" to which Shakespeare was more partial. The quotations from *Troilus and Cressida* and *Richard III* show distaste. The famous passage in *Hamlet* supports the conjecture. It is the "damnable faces" of the murderer that Hamlet objects to, and the "tearing of a passion to tatters" that offends him, i.e. violence of gesture and speech. This protest seems a sincere one, in spite of Granville-Barker's attempt to turn it into a joke because it does not fit in with his theories.

It is important to remember the other plays which the Chamberlain's men staged. They were playing *The Malcontent* at the same time as *Hamlet*, and later they produced *The White Devil*. The acting would not vary very much in quality from one play to another. In a repertory company there is not time to change the method of attack and there is a consequent tendency for the acting to stiffen and become conventional, owing to the strain of having to change the bill frequently (and Shakespeare's company played a different play every day and a new play was produced every month more or less).

A glance at a page of Marston's rhetoric, or Kyd's in *The Spanish Tragedy*, shows that it would have to be delivered quickly, stiffly and with attention to general impressiveness, rather than natural speech emphasis. The wit combats of the comedies and the rough-and-tumble farce need the same method. This was probably why the Elizabethans liked the long sententious speech or the passionate soliloquy. Provided the diction was high-astounding, the delivery must be pompous. Schücking's theory of the

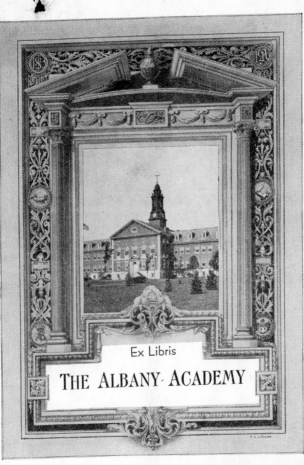

soliloquy as a harangue delivered to the audience would favour this. The aside, too, could not be delivered in a confidential colloquial manner if it were of the long meditative kind; and the bitter punning aside would need to be snapped out in the cut-and-thrust manner of sticho-mythia. The "bravura" speeches, Ophelia on Hamlet's visit, or the Queen on Ophelia's death, would need to be recited rather than acted. Burbage would probably think Hamlet not very different from Hieronimo. There could be no question of Lear as "a tottering old man with a walking stick". It was presumably Burbage's method of delivery that made phrases like "a horse, a horse, my kingdom for a horse", famous.

This is the general consensus of opinion on Elizabethan acting. There would be com-paratively little business, and gesture would be formalised. Conventional movement and heightened delivery would be necessary to carry off the dramatic illusion. If the players spoke in an ordinary voice "they became merely Hum-phrey or Sincklo on the stage of the Globe". When neither scenery nor lighting cut off the characters from their audience and provided the necessary distinction between them, it would have to come from movement, tone and gesture.

The arrangement of characters on the stage was also formal. Processions, dumb shows and battles were effected by judicious grouping. Opposing forces would march in at opposite doors and defy each other: in comedy the speech often demands a visual pattern (e.g. end of Act 4, *A Midsummer Night's Dream*; the discovery scene, *Love's Labour's Lost*). In later plays, Shakespeare introduced pattern when the action had a symbolic value. The scene wherein Cressida is received by the Greeks must have been played almost as a ballet; this emphasises the collective cuckolding of Troilus by his foes, just as earlier the Trojans had been unanimous to keep Helen from Menelaus. The Witches' scenes in *Macbeth* and *Antony and Cleopatra*, 2. 7 and 4. 3, are examples of the same device, which becomes very frequent in the Romances. Certain effects were gained by the use of colour. The heavens were hung with black for tragedies; probably a certain kind of dress indicated that an actor was to be invisible to the rest of the players, for we hear of "gowns to go invisible", and special clothes were provided for ghosts.

How far Shakespeare wrote with his eye on his company it is not easy to tell. T. W. Baldwin, in his elaborate study,[1] has endeavoured to distinguish the parts of various actors, and to prove that Shakespeare built up the parts around them, their age, complexion, height and temper being indicated in the text, and the part made to fit with the snugness of a tailored suit. Sir Edmund Chambers has pointed out that this would mean re-writing if the part was assigned to a different actor at a revival; and the editors of the *New Shakespeare* have discovered two Rosalinds in *As You Like It*, showing that the part was taken by two different boy actors. It is not certain whether the occurrence of actors' names in speech prefixes is due to Shakespeare or the book-keeper.

Plainly Burbage might exercise some influence on Shakespeare's heroes. It is noticeable that they age gradually as he gets older, though he would be playing in the early plays all the time. But this kind of compulsion, like the fashion for Revenge tragedy, is of too general a nature for it to have affected the plays very seriously.

[1] *The Organisation and Personnel of the Shakespearean Company.*

Cleopatra could never have been designed for a particular boy, though his brilliance might have supported Shakespeare. The actors were much more likely to suggest the germ of a part than to shape its final form. It was Shakespeare's habit to begin close to practical necessities, ignore them while he felt enthusiastic, and get out of his difficulties by some kind of "masterly impudence" in the end.

The size of the company would also affect the arrangement of minor parts. The Elizabethan actors were used to doubling two or three parts. Some of the early plays are arranged to be acted by only three or four players. *Julius Caesar* can be played by a company of fifteen; all the conspirators of the first acts become soldiers in the last one. The interest and excitement of *Hamlet* is largely due to the constant stream of new characters. The chief humorous man, for instance, might double Polonius and Osric, and even First Gravedigger. This meant that minor parts were better played; but it made for looseness of construction from the modern point of view, and for episodic plots. The habit seems to have been caused by the public's naïve demand for as many characters in one play as possible, and it must have helped further to separate the actor from his part if the same man appeared in two or three rôles in each performance, without the assistance of more than a primitive make-up to hide his identity. It also explains the ease with which the audience accepted the convention of disguise being impenetrable.

The playwright usually read his play over to the company after the first draughting. They might comment and criticise, or even reject it. There are some grounds for thinking that the dramatist, for the boys' companies at any rate, acted as a kind of producer (Ben Jonson, Induction to *Cynthia's Revels*). We have Shakespeare's irritated testimony that the actors gagged. But this may be merely a hit at Kempe, a privileged person, and a very low comedian, who was famous for making faces, and for his big slippers, as well as his gift of singing and extemporising verses.

The influence of the boy actors would be in favour of an impersonal style of acting. They were carefully trained, and seen at their best in the Court comedy of Lyly, or the equally artificial comedy of Ben Jonson. Shakespeare could not hope to get naturalistic acting from them. Yet he wrote his most delicate verse for them, even in the period when he was mainly interested in developing his prose; there is nothing in *Twelfth Night* as subtle as some of the speeches of Viola.

There is very little "natural" dialogue on the Elizabethan stage, except in bourgeois comedy and tragedy. There are soliloquies, long speeches, lyric passages to be enunciated; and there is sharp-shooting repartee. There is much emotion, delicate and subtle, or passionate, in the verse; but there is little personal, intimate feeling.

It is perhaps a fortunate coincidence that the modern theatre approximates more nearly to its Elizabethan forerunner than to any other. The twentieth century has abolished the picture stage, and except for special purposes of satire or caricature, naturalist scenery is an excrescence. Effects are obtained through lighting and grouping, as those of the Elizabethans were through noise and grouping. Colour and pattern, the effect of procession, and occasionally a formalised manner of speech (e.g. for the asides of expressionist plays) have been adopted. While the modern stage is much more complicated than Shakespeare's in the matter of background, some kind of architectural design usually providing the scene, and in the use of lighting, it is closer to it than anything, except artificial reproductions, which has yet appeared. The value of playing Shakespeare in a vital tradition rather than by archaeological reconstructions compensates for the difference; though certain plays, *A Midsummer Night's Dream* or *The Tempest* for example, still make the background seem garish. But on the whole an occasional travesty is preferable to a level mediocrity.

There is still the danger of experiments like the "Shakespeare in modern dress" fetish. Though the eighteenth century played him in full-bottomed wigs, they did dress very gorgeously in satin and brocade. The Elizabethan actors were famous for their splendid clothes, which definitely helped to cut them off from the audience, and were practically their only means of providing personal distinction, for make-up was very primitive. A parallel sense of splendour can only be obtained by putting Hamlet and Laertes into the Household Cavalry, which introduces further irrelevant suggestions.

There remain two serious dangers: that some actors will misunderstand the kind of interpretation that Shakespeare requires, or that the producer will distort the text in the interest of theatrical effect.

The actor will be puzzled by any lines which he has to speak, but which do not seem to be related to his part. When Fichter as Othello had to say, "It is the cause, it is the cause, my soul", he could discover no meaning in the phrase. He therefore picked up a mirror from Desdemona's dressing table, and looking at his dark reflection, pronounced gloomily, "IT is the cause, IT is the cause, my soul"; and dashed down the glass. The actor wants to make his part human and natural. Even Granville-Barker assumes the attitude of a highly self-conscious, self-analytic individual of the twentieth century; he wants "character" which can be interpreted by the actor (hence his coolness towards Ben Jonson), although he admits that Shakespeare does not provide any in *Love's Labour's Lost*; and Shakespeare's contemporaries wrote plays that would make *Love's Labour's Lost* seem like stark realism.

This interest in "character" is exactly parallel to the attitude of the nineteenth-century critics discussed in an earlier chapter, and fully as anachronistic. It assumes a modern interest in motivation and the psychology of the individual, a desire for morally sympathetic characters, etc. (Sybil Thorndike distorted *Henry VIII* by throwing too much emphasis on Katharine; Sir Henry Irving distorted *The Merchant of Venice* by over-emphasising Shylock; Mrs Siddons *Macbeth* by dwarfing Macbeth.) So Granville-Barker has to slur Hamlet's speech to the players; and when he is confronted by passages like "It is the cause, it is the cause, my soul", or

> ...light thickens, and the crow
> Makes wing to the rooky wood,

which offer no scope to the actor who wishes to put life into his part, he is reduced to calling them "magic". (There is naturally a great deal of magic in *A Midsummer Night's Dream* and all the later plays.)

Moreover, though he himself observed sententiously of the boy companies that "children are children and training is training"—and therefore one can only have the "athletic grace" of impersonal acting from a boy—he has noted that Shakespeare habitually gives his most delicate and subtle verse to the heroines.

This does not prevent irrelevant particularisations. Desdemona, lying about her handkerchief, is "the Venetian lady a little tremblingly on her dignity". This recollection of her origin and status seems to me merely irritating at this point; it reduces the tragedy to a Strong Situation. She might equally well be the hurt child on her dignity, or anything else which by an attempt to assert a power which it does not possess, covers up its own pain, and adds to the pathos of the situation.

The attitude of the actors has changed little since the eighteenth century, when they ruled the stage, and Shakespeare was butchered to provide fatter parts for the principals. The naturalist method of acting still largely prevails; an actor, except in farce, does not "act", but takes the particular kind of part which will allow him to display himself. He is concerned to get as much life (i.e. feeling) into the part as possible. But Shakespeare was not interested in exploiting personal feeling. He ignored innumerable opportunities for touching scenes. No playwright nowadays would stage Ophelia's first interview with Hamlet "off", or Leontes' recognition of Perdita; the audience would want to see it, and the actor to act it. But a piece of descriptive verse was as satisfactory to

Shakespeare's company as a strong scene. The feeling was there, in the verse, just the same. The popularity of Messengers' Speeches has to be borne in mind. Shakespeare did not use them very often (though Enobarbas' description of Cleopatra performs the function of one); but Chapman and Ben Jonson employed them frequently.

Of course Shakespeare was not recited, or mouthed indifferently. The speeches were spoken with passion. But it was not a passion which attempted to reproduce that which an actual person in such a situation would feel; it was not "natural", but more akin to the impersonal art of the ballet-dancer. No one feels for instance, in dialogue, that he is addressing his words to that character to whom he is nominally speaking; the words are spoken partly to oneself, partly to the audience. It is not possible to produce a play by directly exploiting the actors' personalities, but only by reproducing them indirectly, through concentration upon a task "which is a task in the same sense as the making of an efficient engine, or the turning of a jug".[1]

[1] T. S. Eliot in *The Criterion*—"Four Elizabethan Dramatists".

The greed of the actor is usually curbed by the producer, though he allows minor parts to be over-emotionalised to give them "colour". The affection of Hotspur and Lady Percy, for instance, is always excessive on the stage, and as lover-like as Mortimer's sentiment towards his Welsh Lady. The producer can constitute a danger in himself. The author was probably the producer on the Elizabethan stage (though the title dates only from the eighteenth century) and there would be no danger of a rivalry between the two. The producer becomes a fearful wild fowl when he takes the theatre as an independent art. The rise of this very new and very belligerent art means that its rights are asserted with the noisiness of a Suffragette. The polemics of Gordon Craig will not bear quoting; a calmer statement of the case may be cited.

The theatre is an independent and composite art, and appeals through eye and ear, using a number of media such as words, sound, forms, colour, movement in order to convey emotion and idea...the producer is not necessarily an interpretative artist, he is a creative artist...a production is either good theatre art or bad, whether the author's contribution in the way of material and idea be Shakespeare's or Toller's.[1]

[1] Mr Terence Gray in *The Cambridge Review*, 27. ii. 31.

Even an independent and composite art, one would think, would be affected by such a variation in the quality of one of its constituents as is represented by the difference in complexity and delicacy between Shakespeare and a translation of Herr Toller. And even a composite art must start from something: the text is the foundation of the "theatre artist's" production, and therefore will influence his use of "colour", "form" and "movement". He is as "free" as a musician setting words to music. And the more delicate and complex the play, the more the producer will have to efface himself.

The claims of the producer are as dangerous as those of the actor, though they are not so likely at present to lead to mutilation of the text as in the days of Henry Irving, when the producer's interests were in naturalist production. Usually he is unaware of, or uninterested in Shakespeare's stage.

Chapter VIII

SHAKESPEARE'S STAGE AND
HIS POETRY

THE present revival of interest in Shakespeare's stage and his stage craft has been unfortunate in this, that it has taken over without correction the division between his drama and his poetry. Even the most idolatrous critics of last century, who praised Shakespeare for his poetry, considered that their own age had a surer grasp of theatrical technique, i.e. that the values of the contemporary theatre were absolute. Bradley, in his sympathy for those who plead that the "soul" of Shakespearean tragedy is independent of his stage,[1] is postulating a division between "soul" and something grosser, suspiciously akin to the antithesis of Content and Form. A transatlantic scholar puts it more bluntly: "Though the permanent elements of their greatness (i.e. the Elizabethan dramatists') may not indeed have depended upon the equipment and management of their stage, the out-

[1] *Shakespeare's Audience*—Oxford Lectures on Poetry.

ward form and technic of their drama undoubtedly did".[1]

It is precisely the validity of this antithesis which is to be questioned. "The outward form and technic" depended upon the Elizabethan stage far less than that of this century does, because the stage had so little to offer. It provided a neutral background, but it imposed practically no limitations. Each writer could therefore evolve a definite way of using the stage; Ben Jonson's and Heywood's varied far more than do Eugene O'Neill's and Noel Coward's, and both depend on the stage as little as possible. The bareness of their stage forced all good dramatists to evolve a highly personal set of conventions, which might draw little or much on common stock of imagery, incidents and types.

Secondly, the "outward form and technic" is not easily separable from the "permanent elements of their greatness". Efficient plays may be written which are not poetry, or indeed of any literary value, at the present day; but this does not prove that Shakespeare merely wrote poetry plus efficiency of an Elizabethan kind, and that

[1] A. H. Reynolds, *Modern Philology*, 11.

therefore he may succeed poetically where he fails dramatically (as in *Lear*, according to Bradley) or vice versa (as in the co-ordination of the two interests of *Henry IV*), or that a poetic masterpiece could be written in an unsatisfactory form. It is not possible to decorate a structurally efficient play with poetry. The writer of poetic drama is using a medium which is different from and more complex than either poetry or drama. The most dramatic of Elizabethan playwrights is also the most poetic.

The twentieth century has learned to recognise and outwardly to respect the dramatic conventions of the Elizabethans. Like any other conventions, they are justified solely by the uses to which they are put, and when these include *Hamlet*, there is no need to apologise for the conventions. But there is still a tendency to judge unconsciously by twentieth century standards; it is betrayed by the usual opinion that *Othello* is a better constructed play than *Antony and Cleopatra*, or *The Tempest* than *The Winter's Tale*. *The Merry Wives* is a better constructed play than any of them.

Shakespeare's dramatic skill, though recognised, is recognised as a thing apart from his poetry; it apparently makes its effects separately, and its results can be analysed in isolation.

To be effective, drama now asks no more than the drawing of consistent characters, and the logical development of the plot, which is not beyond the technical and mechanical efficiency of Mr Edgar Wallace. A great deal of the emotion is left to the actor to supply, or to particularise; it does not come from the text. In Galsworthy's *Justice*, and O'Neill's *Hairy Ape*, the central scenes have no dialogue at all; they depend entirely on the production and the actor for their effect. (The Elizabethans had an analogy, in the dumb show, which was sometimes allegorical and sometimes represented part of the action, as in the conjuring scenes of *Bussy*, or *The White Devil*. But this was a practice that Shakespeare explicitly rejected; his only use of it is in the later plays, especially *The Tempest*, where he modifies it characteristically.)

The modern playwright uses his technical resources to work directly on the nerves, and produce a state of bodily excitement. *The Emperor Jones* produces a powerful abdominal response, as much akin to literature as the feeling of going up in a lift. It is probable that the use of conjuring, especially realist conjuring, like that in *Faustus* and *The Witch of Edmonton* would produce a similar effect on the Elizabethans; but here again Shakespeare avoids the device, unless the witches in *Macbeth* must be classed with the usual supernaturalism.

Consistency in characterisation and plot, a reproduction of colloquial speech with the consequent prevention of any delicate or precise use of words, are the requisites of most contemporary plays. William Archer judged the Elizabethan drama by these standards, and found it wanting. He politely exempted Shakespeare, but most of his strictures would apply equally well to him. When one of Pinero's characters discovers that the man she loves is already matrimonially provided for, she says to him, "You might have mentioned it". Archer is ecstatic over the dramatic subtlety of this flat little litotes, because it has something of the effect of a double entendre. But he does not see the dramatic point of Tourneur's lines:

Does the silk worm expend her yellow labours
For thee? For thee does she undo herself?

which crystallise all the floating imagery of the *Revenger's Tragedy*, the connections of death and beauty, painted faces and rotting corpses; the futility of pomp ("Sceptre and crown Must tumble down") and the mockery of loveliness and chastity ("Golden lads and lasses must As chimney sweepers, come to dust"), so that Vindice sometimes addresses his mistress as if she had been a courtesan ("Get thee to my lady's chamber, tell her, let her paint an inch thick, to this must she come").

The development of Lear or Macbeth cannot be considered apart from the texture of the words in which it is expressed. The power of implication and of a poetic context may sometimes fill out a phrase in itself as trivial as that of Pinero ("Pray you, undo this button," or "No cause, no cause"). But it is equally often in the poetic implication of the words. "Absent thee from felicity awhile" has the weight of all Hamlet's soliloquies behind it. A more abstract interest in construction allows of "qu'il mourût!" which has the weight of all the conscious structure of the play behind it, and secures that concentration which is the reward of *acknowledged* convention. Shakespeare's structure is largely in his poetry; and therefore the last speech of Hamlet, or some of the speeches of Macbeth in Act 5, have a less deliberate, but more penetrating power than that of Le Vieil Horace.

Shakespeare very seldom depends entirely on the action to produce an effect. He has nothing like the silent scenes of Galsworthy and O'Neill. Usually he avoids this by means of the soliloquy. Brutus and Cassius, in their speeches before their deaths, make their feelings explicit; the effect on the audience does not depend at all on the final act of stabbing themselves. This kind of self-dramatisation was one method of avoiding reliance on mere acting. But the soliloquy can also have the excitement of rapid dialogue or complex action. The debatings of Hamlet or the visions of Macbeth have as much action in them as a combat or a battle. Even in cases where a prolonged description of the character's feelings is not possible, as at the first meeting of Rosalind and Orlando (*As You Like It*, 1. 2, ll. 262–277), they do not turn aside merely with a few embarrassed commonplaces. The words make everything clear; the actors' behaviour will be only a confirmation. "Can I not say, I thank you?—My better parts Are all thrown down..." "Did you call, Sir? Sir, you have wrestled well and overthrown More than your enemies" (compare *Romeo and Juliet*, 1. 5, ll. 116–145, which is much cruder).

Shakespeare's contemporaries were often very naïve in their method of employing this self-descriptive device. The villain would describe his dying pangs with scientific detachment:

> The poison is dispersed through every vein
> And boils like Aetna in my frying guts.

Compare:
> ...I melt, and am not
> Of stronger earth than others.

Shakespeare was equally explicit, but as a rule less direct.

The death scenes offer the best opportunities for this kind of writing. Cleopatra's death is as completely given in her speeches, as her voyage to Cydnus is in the description by Enobarbus. The reported description, like that of Hamlet's visit by Ophelia, or that by the Lord of Cordelia's reception of news of Lear, was excellent practice for a more indirect self-revelation. The Messenger's speech of other tragedians must also be remembered to confirm Shakespeare's practice. The description of the duel in *Bussy* was as good as the duel itself to the Elizabethans.

The neutrality of the Elizabethan stage also meant that Shakespeare had to supply indications of background, and of the passage of time; and this had to be done by poetic means, while the rest of the action was going on. Not often (Ibsen's *Wild Duck* is an exception, with its off-stage garret) does the later playwright attempt this. Shakespeare's background, the Forest of Arden or Lear's Heath where "For miles, there's scarce a bush" are more important than any staging can make them, because they are woven into the play in more complex ways. When scenery is used symbolically in prose, it gives one an unpleasant effect of having been jerked on to a Higher Plane, as in Ibsen's use of the mountains in *Brand, Little Eyolf* and *The Master Builders*. Shakespeare's effect is nearer to that of the novelist, to Hardy's use of Egdon Heath in *The Return of the Native*, for example. The indications of the passage of time are again much more subtle than can be produced by the manipulation of an electric switch, or even by Rebecca West's wearing, in Act 4, the shawl which she was knitting in Act 1. In this delicate use of time, Shakespeare was almost alone among his contemporaries. Marlowe had used it in *Faustus*, and Marston did so spasmodically in *Antonio and Mellida*. It was presumably one of the graces Shakespeare added for himself.

The recognition of the simpler aspects of Shakespeare's technique has led to an examination of its more complicated effects. We recognise, having decided what were *not* his intentions, at what results he aimed, and what means he used. Such books as Mr Noble's *Shakespeare's Use of Song* or Miss Spurgeon's paper on *The Imagery in Shakespearean Tragedy*, are the results of a realisation that his poetry supplied all the effects which a prose dramatist has to separate into technical construction, the recapitulatory method, etc.; that the manipulation of imagery in *Lear* may be the equivalent of the manipulation of exposition in *Ghosts*, that is, the real framework of the play; and that Shakespeare the dramatist was absolutely inseparable from Shakespeare the poet.

Chapter IX

SHAKESPEARE'S STAGE AND
TEXTUAL CRITICISM

THERE are very few places in which an increased knowledge of stage conditions has enabled editors to emend an obscure passage in Shakespeare. The business was so definitely subordinated to gesture and speech, that it hardly ever supplied more than a very subsidiary effect (the recognition of Cordelia by Lear is perhaps the most obvious exception). The low comedy benefits most, as might be expected.

The influence of the study of the stage upon questions of the history and authenticity of the text is, however, much more active. The new school of bibliographical criticism has used its researches to reconstruct customs of the playhouse, on which the history of the manuscript depends. It has in turn been influenced by such evidence as the historians of the stage have collected. The work of Pollard, Dover Wilson and their school depends largely on the economy of the playhouse, and the practice of the players with regard to prompt copy, parts and "plots". In this indirect way, the traditions of the theatre have reacted very potently upon the text through the theories of assembled texts, of Bad Quartos, and the validity of readings taken from them, and the relative merits of Quarto and Folio. Here the exuberance of discovery is still liable to lead to a certain rashness in jumping to conclusions, and the intolerable deal of deduction produced from every pennyworth of evidence offers a ready target for the more sardonically minded.

Any attempt to reconstruct the staging of a particular play is necessarily bound up with its textual history. The stage directions will vary in fullness according to the kind of manuscript from which the play was printed. *Romeo and Juliet* depends on a Bad Quarto and a Good Quarto, which represent different methods of presentation, as well as different versions of the text. Possibly this was a more effective way of disguising an old play than getting Shakespeare to pad out the manuscript; and it would certainly be easier for the actors to introduce new business rather than to learn new lines.

It is assumed by the bibliographers that the

players duplicated their play as little as possible for fear of pirate printers, though, as Chambers remarks, they seem to have taken little care to keep the one copy out of pirates' hands. This has led to the cheering probability that some of the Good Quartos and the new plays in the Folio were set up from Shakespeare's own manuscript, which, having been endorsed by the Master of the Revels, served at once as "allowed book", and prompt copy.

Interpolations were written into the same manuscript, or on small slips which were pasted into it; deletions, marked by brackets, sometimes got into print. We have, for instance, two accounts of Romeo's death, and two of the death of Portia in *Julius Caesar*, which are clearly alternate versions. (Incidentally, textual criticism has here disposed of a moral problem. Brutus's apparent dissimulation perturbed the critics considerably.) But the doctrine of "continuous copy" leads to some curious results in the case of revised plays. It is necessary to assume that *Hamlet* retains odd and accidental traces of Kyd, which almost suggest that Shakespeare made a palimpsest over the old play.

The danger that the loss of this single copy would entail is obvious. It is known that the book of *The Winter's Tale* was lost, for instance. In this case the bibliographers assume the theory of an assembled text, made by putting the players' parts together, and adding stage directions from the plot or skeleton of the action, which hung in the tiring house. Such a piece of work would be very difficult, and owing to the shortness of cues it might lead to misplaced speeches; this, however, is not a feature of such of Shakespeare's plays (*The Two Gentlemen, Merry Wives, The Winter's Tale*) as are considered to be assembled texts.

The Bad Quartos provide the most fascinating work for the literary detective. They are garbled versions of the plays, surreptitiously printed, but the nature of their garbling is so extraordinary that it is difficult to account for it by any single hypothesis. The first theory, that they were early versions simply, is inadequate. A second theory of a copyist in the audience who took down a shorthand version, would not account for the misplacements and misnamings of characters, though it would for the full descriptive stage directions. A traitorous actor who dictated the play might explain the comparative excellence of certain scenes and parts. Mr Lawrence has recently suggested that the Bad Quartos were cut-down versions prepared for a travelling company, and Mr Alexander also believes that they were later adaptations from a better text.

Even the punctuation is now explained as "rhetorical rather than logical", i.e. it is explained in terms of the theatre and the actor, and is therefore restored to a position of authority.

The *New Shakespeare* is the first edition to embody the results of modern research. Shakespeare has been freed from act and scene division, the interpolations of the Folio and of Rowe. The dramatic quality of the play is emphasised by full stage directions, which attempt to provide a substitute for a performance. Here, perhaps, the tendency to visualise a scene too precisely still shows traces of nineteenth-century realist staging. It is possible that the scene of *The Tempest* may have been "a green platt of undercliff, approached by a path descending through a grove of lime trees alongside the upper cliff, in the face of which is an entrance to a tall cave, curtained"; though to bring the lime trees here on the evidence of 5. 5, l. 10

seems to emphasise them unduly. Shakespeare refers to them there because he needed some such property, but they might well be "off", and it is not likely that he constantly visualised them as part of the *mise en scène*. It is less likely that *The Merchant of Venice*, 5. 1, was "the avenue before Portia's house at Belmont, A Summer Night: The moon with drifting clouds". If these stage directions are a cue to the reader to "work his thoughts", i.e. if they are meant for the imagination only, they are superseded by the poetry which follows; if they are real descriptions of the *mise en scène*, they are too precise. (And why drifting clouds? I cannot find them in the bond.)

The *New Shakespeare* has also dropped the eighteenth-century habit of "regarding the punctuation as wholly within its power", and so has restored some delicate readings. But it has adopted a Marconi-like system of dots and dashes in place of the Elizabethan stops, which were the same as ours, but had not the same values; and this is inclined to give it the appearance of a film caption.

The full implications of textual free thought and dangers of the new rationalism are displayed in the Notes on the Copy for each play. Not a single play is left in a condition of finality and integrity. *The Tempest* bears suggestions of an earlier play, and of a subsequent abridgment by Shakespeare. *The Two Gentlemen* is an assembled text, much cut down, and with adaptations by somebody else; it is also founded on an older play. *Measure for Measure* has been both abridged and expanded by a second hand, and adapted by Shakespeare for the Court. *Love's Labour's Lost* has been revised by Shakespeare, and is based on an older, non-Shakespearean play. *The Merchant of Venice* is from a prompt book made up of assembled parts, revised by Shakespeare and also founded on an older play. *As You Like It* has "undergone a drastic revision" by Shakespeare, and the masque of Hymen is by somebody else. *All's Well* has been adapted by the collaborator of *Measure for Measure* and *As You Like It*. The rest of Shakespeare's plays are in like state; they are a sorry sight, and they might, like Achilles' Myrmidons,

Noseless, handless, hacked, and chipped, come to him
Crying on...

unknown revisers, the actors, Heminge and Condell, and Jaggard and all his devils.

So far only the comedies have been issued in this edition; and most of them have hitherto been considered straightforward texts. Exciting things may be expected of *Macbeth*, *Timon* and *Troilus and Cressida*.

The difficulties which are pointed out are real enough. It is only the conclusions with which quarrel can be sought, and these are not offered as in any sense final. Some of the suggestions, one may think, have been advanced because of their ingenuity rather than their plausibility. The excitement of settling such questions is akin to the pleasure of solving a crossword puzzle, or fathoming a detective mystery; finality is not to be resisted.

The even more speculative and hazardous labours of the professional disintegrators are also based upon a reconstruction of playhouse custom, though the appeal to a "sense of style" is their usual justification. The various theories of revision, collaboration and interpolation must in the first place be deduced from the plays themselves. We know little of the methods of collaborators, and then chiefly those of Henslowe's hacks. The special case of the "Beaumont and Fletcher" plays has never received adequate investigation. On questions of revision and interpolation, there is practically no outside information, and speculation is consequently quite unfettered. Even so old a student of the drama as Mr Lawrence could recently suggest that collaborators always used the act as a unit.[1]

These questions are related very nearly to the actual conditions of the stage. It was the size of the playhouses and the smallness of the theatre-going public which made quick changes of bill necessary, and drove playwrights to collaborate for speed, and to cobble old plays by the addition of a few topical allusions or an expansion of the more popular parts. The frequency with which this kind of research invents theatrical custom detracts a little from the value of its results. The danger of borrowing an avowedly "scientific" method for questions which depend on style, on the quality of language, is obvious; but it seems to have been largely overlooked. The valuable results which scientific methods have achieved when applied to the history of the stage are perhaps unfortunate in that they suggest something equally positive may be obtained by applying them to the drama. In their marshalling of word lists, their rather mechanical

[1] *Pre-Restoration Stage Studies.*

[140]

vocabulary tests and verbal parallels, and their very rigid conceptions of prosody, the methods of J. M. Robertson and Mr Dugdale Sykes are too reminiscent of those which have been successfully applied elsewhere to quite different material, by W. J. Lawrence, for instance. The battle cry of Robertson is "science", but he does not seem to conceive that a scientific tape measure may be inadequate as an instrument for measuring poetry.

The "game of parallels" is particularly pernicious and here, perhaps, the disintegrators might profit from a more frequent reference to theatrical conditions. It is possible, in the case of a playwright like Shakespeare, who was also an actor, and must have had many parts by heart, and whole plays half by heart (as the Piratical Actor, if he is not a myth, had); it is possible that such parallels may be due to recent revivals of the plays from which they are taken. A study of Shakespeare's borrowings from the known repertory of the Globe might be illuminating.

The discovery of exactly how much licence there was on the Elizabethan stage, and how little respect for the text of a play, has led to a great irresponsibility towards the surviving versions. Emendations are more lightly proposed when it is realised that we have no authoritative text, as sacrosanct and final as Moses' tables of the law, but merely one version of a fluid and changing substance, which may or may not be the author's final one. Anything which is not immediately intelligible can easily be credited to survivals of an earlier version, writing which is not up to the level of the rest to another hand. Even Shakespeare's technical devices are mistaken for crudities in the desire to find evidence of a seamy side to the text. Some of the little references in which he indulges, to happenings "off" or unknown characters (like Claribel and the Duke of Milan's son in *The Tempest*, the Hermit in *The Merchant of Venice*, 5. 1, etc.) are meant to give an impression of the dramas being really a slice of life, of things going on outside the framework of the play; but they are usually described as fossils of an earlier story or indications of a change of plan. This is perhaps better than regarding them as serious problems (Bradley's note on the Hermit can be well imagined), but it is an example of the dangers of literal reading, and the critical myopia which a too long staring at the text will breed.

It is known that plays were very often carelessly put together and were really no more unified than a revue. *The Two Lamentable Tragedies* consists of two quite detachable stories; this practice of divided plot and sub-plot increased in the decadent late Jacobean and Caroline theatre. Dekker hastily puts Jonson and himself, disguised as Romans, into a Norman Court. But Shakespeare never does this kind of thing. The two worlds of *Cymbeline* produce an effect from their juxtaposition, like that of the Court and the Country in pastoral poetry, and not very different from some functions of metaphor. Nor is it likely that Shakespeare found much pleasure in botching his own old plays or other people's. In the same time he could have written a new one. And the particular kind of revision with which he is usually credited is particularly unprofitable. Expansion of minor parts and the addition of new scenes might be acceptable to the actors and obvious to the audience; but to re-write the main speeches would mean that the actors had to re-learn their parts, which were yet not much augmented, and the difference would be hardly perceptible to the audience.

Chapter X

CONCLUSION

THE new tendencies in Shakespearean criticism, if sometimes disquieting, are always exciting, and their main direction is healthy. They depend at least on a close attention to the text. Theories are required to have some foundation in fact. There is a demand for evidence; and evidence is forthcoming in such quantities that some time will be needed to digest it. Meanwhile the excitement grows, controversies rise, and are much to be preferred to a dreary and uncontested chorus of adulation. Ferocity has returned to Shakespearean criticism. Nearly every critic has some personal theory, for which he indulges in special pleading. The forensic methods of Schücking and J. M. Robertson may warp their judgment and over-colour their style ("the blood pressure rises", as the last critic has said of one of his particular enemies) but they sharpen the wits, rouse up the spirits, and have most of the virtues of Falstaff's sherris-sack.

CONCLUSION

The tendency on the whole is to rationalise Shakespeare. To the eighteenth century he was a Noble Savage, an inexplicable phenomenon, acting by the light of nature. The nineteenth century insisted that his judgment was equal to his genius; but that he must not be approached critically, "Others abide our question, thou art free". The rich and untidy nature of his genius was recognised but not acknowledged. The twentieth century has questioned him.

The questioning is sometimes dangerous when it results in premature rigidity. The textual critics are prone to elaborate theories, and to desire more conclusive results than are possible. An example of this is Percy Simpson's theory of punctuation, which explained the stops as rhetorical rather than logical. He began by considering it as a definite system, but he has since modified his views considerably, though the punctuation has permanently gained in prestige. But all roughness of the text is explained by the exigencies of the theatre; no difficulties are allowed to be fundamental, no obscurities to be deliberate. Shakespeare is explained with a completeness that in itself provokes scepticism. This is partly due to the humility of the scholar, who, while separating himself from the critic, has now to deal with specifically literary matters. The danger is that Shakespeare will be thought of too much in terms of the theatre alone.

The critics of dramatic structure are equally inclined to scientific methods. A certain phenomenon will be christened the Law of Reentry and will at once acquire a dignified status and a conscious recognition that the Elizabethans certainly did not bestow on it. They would not recognise the Objective Truth of Soliloquies, even if it were explained to them; there was no conscious formulation of the dramatic code, for the neo-classic Rules were the official creed. The exceptions which Stoll and Schücking are compelled to make to their self-created rules are the best criticism of their methods. They are too anxious to ascribe a system to Shakespeare, to tabulate his methods, and to explain his productions in terms of their first motivating factor, though these explain the other playwrights just as much or as little as he. Their logic and their admirable but limited rationalism often remind the reader of Rymer; they seem to be endeavouring to build an

Elizabethan Creed which shall rival the neo-classic rules in precision and inviolability.

The disintegrators, on the other hand, are impelled by an excessive veneration which will not hear of Shakespeare's having written a poor line. If Stoll is the progeny of Rymer, Robertson is the vivacious and vigorous offspring of Coleridge, who would have given the Porter's speech in *Macbeth* to a base collaborator, but retained the single sentence about the primrose path, which pleased him, for Shakespeare's own. It is greatly to the credit of Dr Johnson that, though he was profoundly shocked by Shakespeare's puns, and by Lady Macbeth's references to "the blanket of the dark" and other vulgar household properties, he did not take refuge in the barbarism of Shakespeare's age or in theories of collaboration.

There is much that is transient and of his own age, which any writer will take for granted, and his ways of feeling and thought, his methods of expression will be determined by it. The drama is peculiarly dependent on external influences, and the influence of the age is consequently increased. The business of getting to know an author is largely that of learning the implications of his personal code, his specialised uses of structure and words; and, in the case of a dramatist, this will depend on his theatre and his audience. Continual and sensitive reading does much to assist the reader, but it cannot do everything to enable him to complete this essential task. The value of the study of Elizabethan stage conditions lies in this elucidation of the author's methods. It will largely be negative; it will prevent the interference of the unconscious preconceptions of our own age, the most fruitful source of irrelevant criticism. (The absorption of Elizabethan materials is bound to be conscious, but the learning of Shakespeare's technique, since it is primarily a poetic one, i.e. dependent on his use of words, will usually be unconscious.) A study of his age will also discourage the purely personal and appreciative criticism which consists of the creation of an inferior kind of private poem.

Historic criticism is a reversal of the synthetic creative process; its duty is to disentangle and unravel all the knit-up feelings, to split the compound into its elements. What is left is not the play; but it tells us a great deal about the play. This kind of work is not appreciative criticism; the two studies are complementary, and therefore necessary to everyone who would approach Shakespeare, but they must be kept apart, or a bastard criticism like the scientific-stylistic efforts of Robertson result. The critic must know something of the history of *Hamlet* as a play to understand it, but he must not use his knowledge in his final judgment, though it may have limited the field over which his judgment is extended.

The critic must, in fact, cultivate the detachments of the Elizabethans. As they judge the one character separately as hero and as villain, yet recognise him all the while for one man, so Shakespeare must be seen both within his period and without it; as being both "of an age" and "for all time".